Frances Akinde

BE AN ALLY, NOT A BYSTANDER

TEACHING ALLYSHIP LESSONS IN PRIMARY SCHOOLS

CORWIN

A SAGE Publishing Company

1 Oliver's Yard
55 City Road
London EC1Y 1SP

2455 Teller Road
Thousand Oaks
California 91320

Unit No 323-333, Third Floor, F-Block
International Trade Tower,
Nehru Place, New Delhi – 110 019

8 Marina View Suite 43-053
Asia Square Tower 1
Singapore 018960

Editor: Amy Thornton
Editorial assistant: Iris Kwok
Production editor: Chris Marke
Marketing manager: Dilhara Attygalle
Cover design: Wendy Scott
Typeset by: C&M Digitals (P) Ltd, Chennai, India
Printed and bound by CPI Group (UK) Ltd, Croydon, CR0 4YY

Library of Congress Control Number: 2024936855

British Library Cataloguing in Publication data

A catalogue record for this book is available from the British Library

ISBN 978-1-0719-2890-5
ISBN 978-1-0719-2889-9 (pbk)

CONTENTS

ABOUT THE AUTHOR

Frances Akinde is a former headteacher of a secondary special school (11–19) for learners with autism and associated difficulties and a qualified Special Educational Needs Coordinator (SENCO). Over the last 20 years, Frances has worked in a variety of roles across primary, secondary, special/alternative provision and local authority, from art/design technology teacher to an SLCN advisory teacher liaising with speech and language therapists across a local authority.

After discovering in her 40s that she was neurodivergent and had a hearing impairment, Frances decided to use her lived experiences to offer training and support to ensure that our schools and workplaces are truly inclusive.

In January 2023, Frances co-launched BAMEed SEND hub as part of the BAMEed Network, a diverse network for educators which aims to ensure diversity and address racial inequities in education.

She is an 'Anti-Racist Schools' award coach for Leeds Beckett University, enabling schools to evaluate overall anti-racism support and strategies that exist within their school, while also helping to give structure to the development plan for any improvements.

As a neurodivergent educator, Frances uses her experiences to support and mentor people who may be struggling in the workplace and in education.

DEDICATION AND ACKNOWLEDGEMENTS

DEDICATION

This book is for everyone. Everyone who believes that the experiences we go through shape who we are and how we show up in the world.

These experiences influence not only how we raise our children but also how we teach others. As educators, we have a huge responsibility to do our very best to demonstrate how to be active global citizens and, in turn, teach the next generation what allyship truly looks like.

In writing this book, I hope that all children will be able to show up as their whole selves, confident that they have our support to do so.

As Maya Angelou said, 'When you know better, you do better.' As educators, we don't always get things right, but we must commit to change. I hope this book helps you to do just that. By learning about ourselves, we learn how to change, and through kindness and compassion, we can teach our children to be good humans.

After all, how do you change the world? This often begins with an individual who, through one person at a time, creates a ripple effect that leads to change.

I dedicate this book to the giants who came before me, the allies and advocates worldwide, past and present; they have paved the way for us.

I would, in particular, like to thank my family, friends, and every individual who has shown up for me when I needed them most. That is true allyship.

Lastly, I would like to dedicate this book to the wonderful year six classes of Pelham Primary School and Fairford Academy Barnehurst, who inspired me to write this book.

ACKNOWLEDGEMENTS

First and foremost, I acknowledge myself and all the sacrifices I have made to finish this book! On a serious note, it has been hard, and there were many times that my brain just wanted to switch off! But fortunately, I am stubborn, and I like a challenge. This book has been my therapy over the last few months, so it meant too much to me to give up.

My work as an assistive technology trainer gave me access to tools that helped me bring my ideas to life. This book would not have been written without these and the support of my editor, Amy Thornton, my development editor, Ruth Lilly and my assistive technology trainer, Tim, at D&A.

This book also wouldn't have been possible without the brilliant books on Allyship and the Bystander Effect that came before it, from the holy books of the past to the personal accounts of allyship from modern-day authors.

In addition, a whole community of people have supported me, both in real life and on social media, so I need to acknowledge them, too. Throughout this book, I have tried to acknowledge them all.

FOREWORD FROM THE AUTHOR

It's summer 2023. I'm a year out of my headship of a special school for learners with autism and associated difficulties and reflecting on the year that's gone by. I would never have imagined a year ago that I would be sitting here in the summer holidays, planning out a book, *my* book on allyship.

But over the past year, I have seen so many examples of people being a bystander when they should have been an ally and I have been determined to use my personal experience to ensure change. As adults, we find it difficult to change. We become so set in our ways that we find it hard to deviate from them. But to me, being an educator, a role I have had for over 20 years, is not only about developing the younger generations, but also re-educating and improving ourselves and the people around us. When faced with the choice of whether to think of others or ourselves, allyship is an opportunity for us to show up, be upstanders and model the correct way of being.

When I left headship, I didn't know what I was going to do in the future. I didn't know what my trajectory would look like because it was so different from what I had planned. There were people that I needed to be my allies, that decided to be bystanders instead. That's not how I was brought up.

Your first allies are your family. They are often the closest support we have. We are meant to be able to depend on our families, especially during challenging times. Unfortunately, though, not everyone has a positive or supportive family. Instead of being allies, they may stand by when their children are exposed to harm and not take the steps they should to protect them. For this reason, some people find that allies come from outside their immediate family. I am care experienced. I was fostered from the age of 3-13 alongside my younger sister. That experience taught me that your family is not just your blood. Children in my household were not related to me and often they would come and go, but they were family. We looked out for each other and made sure everyone was okay. Our parents weren't around to do it, we had no choice.

So, when I became an educator, working with children presenting with challenging behaviour, it was my job to be an ally to them, to advocate for them, to ensure that they got everything they needed not only to get a good education as a basic right, but to go beyond that, to support them to thrive. The painful experience of realising that people would not always show up for me, made me even more determined to teach children from a young age how to show up for other people when they needed them.

I hope you find this book useful, and more importantly, I hope it makes a lasting impact on both you and your students. After all, how do we change the world? Through one person at a time.

Frances Akinde

INTRODUCTION: WHY A BOOK ABOUT ALLYSHIP?

When you are made to feel different just for being you.

When you are treated as if your identity is less important than someone else's.

When you highlight discrimination and the pain this causes, and you're not believed.

It hurts.

BE AN ALLY, NOT A BYSTANDER

In recent years, we have seen a rise in hate crimes, isolation, loneliness and societal exclusion. According to the Home Office figures, the number of hate crimes recorded by police in England and Wales rose by 26 per cent to 155,841 in the year to March 2022. More than two-thirds of all hate crimes reported were race-related (Nagesh, 2022). Since the pandemic, we have also experienced lasting negative economic, political and social consequences of the response to the pandemic, which has increased xenophobic and racist attitudes and associated hate crimes as people look for others to blame (Luthra and Nandi, 2022).

Isolation and loneliness are both also significant issues that the pandemic has exacerbated.

The content in *Be An Ally, Not A Bystander* supports the guidance around relationship education, specifically friendships, family relationships and respecting others. This component of the guidance aims to help children develop strong, healthy relationships and understand how to handle different emotions and situations.

We need to create inclusive communities where everyone feels welcome and valued. We need to create that sense of togetherness and belonging; what better place to model that than in our school communities?

WHY IS THIS IMPORTANT?

As good educators and loving parents/carers, we would not want our children to suffer. Yet, discrimination, which is often described as 'like death by a 1000 cuts', is something that sadly we may not always be able to protect our children and young people from. The least we can do is prepare them for it so they are better able to protect themselves

When I started to run workshops and training sessions in schools around allyship, it was because I realised that a sense of advocacy, community and belonging needs to start from childhood. It became evident to me that the most important thing we can do to change the world is to ensure that all our children are taught to be allies from a young age.

If we form the idea of allyship in their hearts during their crucial years of development, those concepts and values will likely stick throughout their lives. We create change and lasting impact by nurturing, in particular, the concepts of kindness, compassion and care from an early age. Fostering these values is at the core of allyship. By cultivating these ideas, we lay the foundation for change.

As an educator, having the opportunity to hold space for children to share what being an ally means to them and how people have shown up for them has been one of the greatest privileges of my teaching career. Educators play a vital role in shaping young minds; they are more than teachers, and their role goes beyond transmitting information. Educators shape the foundation upon which a child's understanding of the world is built. Through nurturing relationships and classrooms, we can create an environment where curiosity flourishes, questions are encouraged, and students feel empowered to express themselves without fear of discrimination.

LACK OF RESOURCES

One of the reasons I began to write this book was because, although allyship is explicitly mentioned regarding 'LGBTQ+ allyship' and inclusive relationships under 'relationship and sex education', I could not find many curriculum resources explicitly on allyship, prejudice and anti-racism. It's crucial to have comprehensive materials that encompass all aspects of allyship and promote inclusivity.

COVERING THE STATUTORY DFE CONTENT GUIDANCE

The Department for Education (DfE) provides *Relationships Education, Relationships and Sex Education (RSE) and Health Education* statutory guidance (published June 2019 and last updated September 2021) for schools to deliver age-appropriate and comprehensive education on relationships, sex and health to children and young people (DfE, 2021a). Relationships education has been compulsory for pupils in England's primary education phase since September 2020. At the time of publication, relationships, sex and health education (RSHE) was being reviewed, with updated guidelines expected in 2024.

The statutory requirement to provide health education does not apply to independent schools – PSHE is already compulsory, as independent schools must meet the Independent School Standards, as set out in the *Education (Independent School Standards) Regulations 2014* (DfE, 2019). The guidance emphasises the importance of making the curriculum inclusive and respecting different cultures, backgrounds and beliefs while remaining age appropriate. In particular, 'Schools should ensure that the policy meets the needs of pupils and parents and reflects the community they serve' (DfE, 2021a, p. 11). It also stresses the importance of delivering the content around relationships and sex education (RSE) sensitively and respectfully, allowing students to engage in open discussions.

Relationships education, RSE and health education must be accessible to all pupils. The DfE guidance states, 'in teaching Relationships Education and RSE, schools should ensure that the needs of all pupils are appropriately met and that all pupils understand the importance of equality and respect' (DfE, 2021a, p. 15).

Although the guidance does not explicitly mention 'allyship' and 'bystanders' as standalone topics, these concepts are in line with the broader content around promoting respect, inclusivity and positive relationships, which align with the principles of allyship and the role of the bystander in preventing harm and promoting positive behaviour.

REFLECTION

As educators, we are role models, demonstrating empathy, respect and open-mindedness. We must listen when children and peers tell us about their experiences. Just because we may not be able to relate to something personally does not mean that it didn't happen in the way that person describes it. This is where empathy is important, acknowledging another individual's feelings, even if other members of the same group interpret things in different ways. Creating a secure base within our classrooms and wider schools is vital for connection, correction and exploration so that students can thrive as individuals, ready to contribute positively to society.

Show your children that you are their first and strongest ally by committing to act when made aware of discrimination and following up. It takes bravery, confidence and courage to be open about bullying, harassment and discrimination, and children may not know the right way to open up about these experiences.

FURTHER READING AND RESOURCES

This book is not designed to be used as a scheme of work. However, it can be dipped into in response to incidences and linked to the PSHE Association curriculum planning frameworks as a relevant resource.

The PSHE Association has many helpful resources that complement the content of this book, available at:

https://pshe-association.org.uk/guidance/ks1-5/handling-complex-issues-safely-classroom

BULLYING AND DISCRIMINATION

In addition, several charities offer support around these key themes.

The Runnymede Trust: This UK-based think tank focuses on racial equality and social justice. It provides research reports and resources related to racism and discrimination in the UK.

Show Racism the Red Card: This organisation offers educational resources to tackle racism, initially through football. It provides lesson plans and materials suitable for schools.

Stephen Lawrence Foundation: Named after Stephen Lawrence, a Black British teenager murdered in a racially motivated attack in 1993, this foundation works towards a fairer and more inclusive society. It offers educational resources and workshops.

Local authority initiatives: Some local councils, such as Brighton, Hampshire and Haringey, have specific resources related to anti-racism and diversity education. It's worth checking with your local education authority for support.

Black History Month UK: Explore the resources and events associated with Black History Month in the UK, which often include educational materials and activities.

Anne Frank Trust UK: This organisation provides educational resources and workshops on the Holocaust, prejudice and discrimination. It aims to promote tolerance and understanding.

UK Parliament's Education Service: The UK Parliament offers educational resources that include lessons on democracy, equality and human rights. These can be integrated into discussions about prejudice and discrimination.

Equality and Human Rights Commission (EHRC): EHRC guides teaching equality and human rights in schools. It offers resources designed to help educators promote equality and diversity.

In contrast to the government in England, the Scottish government has released a whole bank of resources to support schools to develop an anti-racist curriculum, available at: https://education.gov.scot/resources/breaking-the-mould-principles-for-an-anti-racist-curriculum

Wales has taken action to become an anti-racist nation, also producing a range of resources covering children's rights to equality and non-discrimination as part of its Anti-Racist Wales Action Plan. They include classroom resources, booklets and videos, available at: www.childcomwales.org.uk/equality-and-anti-racism-resources/

Ireland has also launched a National Action Plan Against Racism, available at: www.gov.ie/en/publication/14d79-national-action-plan-against-racism/

It just leaves England to catch up. This book is designed to help us do just that.

1

PRE-DELIVERY WORK: DOING THE INNER WORK IN ORDER TO DO THE OUTER WORK

KEY CONCEPTS

The key concepts covered in this chapter are:

- establishing what we mean by privileges;
- the importance of reflecting on our personal privileges;
- how we can best use awareness of personal privileges to model good allyship to our pupils.

INTRODUCTION

Working within diversity, equality, inclusion and justice is not easy work. It's essential to give ourselves space to reflect on our own experiences, thoughts and feelings. However, looking inward is not always easy, especially if, like me, you have had some negative experiences where people did not show up for you or where you know you could have been a better ally and friend. But being able to reflect is essential. Giving yourself the space to analyse your past behaviours helps us better understand ourselves and the world we all inhabit.

We all have different realities based on our backgrounds and experiences. We cannot educate our children/young people without educating, reflecting and re-educating ourselves. Being able to have conversations about our biases, the way we have discriminated against others and our own privileges requires us to be self-aware, open to listening and willing to learn. Let's start with privileges.

WHAT ARE PRIVILEGES?

We all have privileges. These are unearnt advantages or benefits. I recognise that I have privileges. My privileges are that I have access to quality education, which has opened up better job opportunities. I also speak English fluently, making it easier to communicate in English-speaking countries. Living in the UK means I can access free healthcare and medicine is easy to obtain. I have fewer challenges as a heterosexual female, and my gender identity matches my assigned sex at birth.

The other side is the barriers I face because of my protected characteristics. You cannot see all of them.

I am **Black,** so I do not benefit from white privilege. White privilege is the benefit people who are racialised as white may experience due to systemic bias towards them and historical superiority due to western colonialism and other historical oppressions such as apartheid.

I am a biological **female,** so I don't benefit from the advantages males may experience over females such as those seen in gender pay gaps. In some countries, girls and women are still not allowed to have access to education; they have limited career opportunities and decision-making power. I live in a country where women and girls have equal rights protected by law, but this is not the case around the world, and I still face barriers to opportunity as a Black woman.

I am **disabled**; my hearing impairment means that without my hearing aid, I would find it harder to navigate social communication. I have the privilege of living in a country where my hearing is regularly checked, and I am given a hearing aid and replacement batteries for free.

This removes some barriers for me as, without my hearing aid, taking part in conversations and understanding others would be more difficult. I use accessibility tools such as captions during online meetings and, as I am not entirely deaf, I can access most of the spoken word. If I were profoundly deaf in both ears, I would struggle with hearing the world without sign language, being able to lip read or having people's voices amplified for me through technology.

I am **neurodiverse**. My diagnosis of dyslexia and ADHD means that I struggle with processing information and concentrating on one task at a time. Without assistive technology such as word processing and dictation I would have struggled to write this book, and with other challenges such as organising my thoughts and myself.

Part of being an ally is acknowledging how our privileges affect our understanding of the experiences of others; we can only see from our own lens, so it's essential to personally reflect on our own privileges as this affects how we see the world and judge other people's experiences.

My experiences of discrimination and bias are why I am passionate about allyship. When I try to explain my experiences, people do not always understand. Sometimes, they are just not willing to listen.

The earlier we teach about the concept of privilege, the easier it becomes to understand.

WHY IS THIS IMPORTANT?

It is essential to go back to the core aim of this book and how you will use your reflections to help your students grow in confidence to move from being bystanders to active allies. Making authentic connections with the work will, in turn, help foster greater understanding for your students as they will see that you are truly invested in change.

First and foremost, it's essential to recognise our own privileges. There are lots of misconceptions about this concept. Privilege does not mean apologising for being a dominant group. However, recognising our positions of power and how we can use these to support other social groups is the ultimate demonstration of allyship.

PAUSE FOR SELF-REFLECTION

What are your privileges? Use the 'Privilege pie' diagram (shown in Figure 1.1) to map out your own privileges.

- What are your personal feelings about your own privileges?
- What would you add to your pie?

(Continued)

- How many slices do you have?
- Share your pie diagram with others and discuss your privileges with them.
- How do you think these affect the way you are able to show up in our world? What advantages do you have because of your privileges?
- What have you learnt from doing this task?

EXPLORING OUR SELF-AWARENESS OF OUR PRIVILEGES?

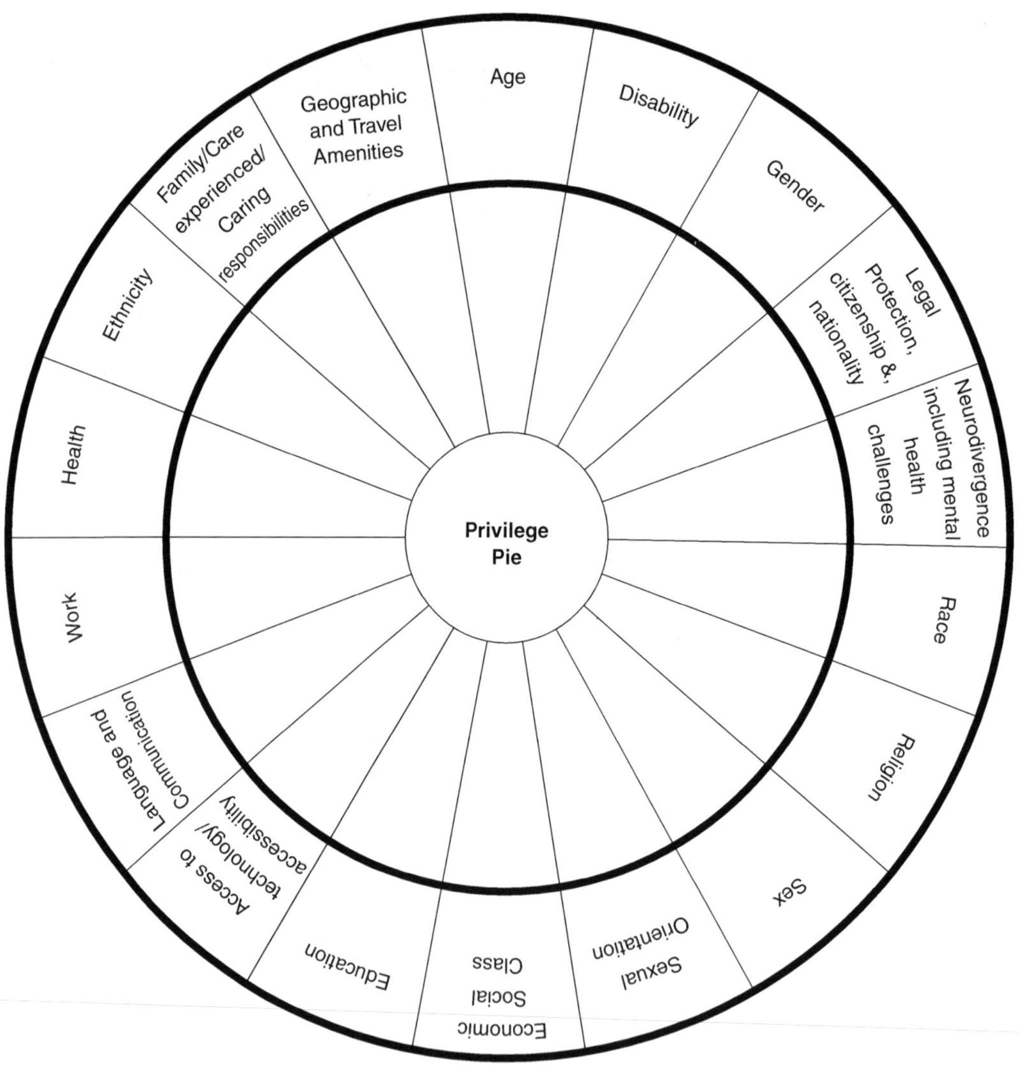

Figure 1.1 Privilege pie

Inspired by Kimberlé Crenshaw's work on Intersectionality. Adapted from *Intersecting axes of privilege, domination, and oppression*. Morgan, 1996 [27] (p.107)

1. **Age:** Consider how your age may impact your opportunities and advantages in society compared to individuals of different age groups.
2. **Disability:** Reflect on whether you have physical, sensory, cognitive, or emotional disabilities and how this may affect your access to services, employment and overall quality of life.
3. **Gender:** Consider the privileges or disadvantages of your gender identity and how it may impact your experiences, opportunities and societal expectations.
4. **Legal protection, citizenship and nationality:** Reflect on whether you have legal protections, citizenship rights, or benefits based on your nationality and how this may affect your access to resources and opportunities.
5. **Neurodivergence, including mental health challenges:** Consider whether you have any neurodivergent conditions or mental health challenges and how this may shape your experiences and access to support.
6. **Race:** Reflect on your racial background and consider the privileges or disadvantages associated with it in terms of systemic racism, discrimination and access to opportunities.
7. **Religion:** Consider whether you belong to a particular religion or are part of a religious majority or minority and how this may impact your social acceptance, access to services and freedom to practice your beliefs.
8. **Sex:** Reflect on the privileges or disadvantages associated with being male, female, or with a gender identity that differs from your assigned sex at birth and how this may affect your treatment, expectations and societal norms.
9. **Sexual orientation:** Consider your sexual orientation and reflect on the privileges or disadvantages associated with it in terms of acceptance, legal protections and social relationships.
10. **Economic social class:** Reflect on your socioeconomic status and consider the privileges or disadvantages that come with it, such as access to education, healthcare, housing and employment opportunities.
11. **Education:** Consider the level of education you have attained and how it may impact your access to higher-paying jobs, social mobility and overall opportunities.
12. **Access to technology:** Reflect on your access to technology, including internet access, devices and digital literacy, and how it may influence your participation in the digital age and access to information and services.

13. **Language and communication:** Consider whether you are a native speaker of a globally dominant language and how it may provide advantages in communication, education and access to resources.
14. **Work:** Reflect on your occupation, job security and workplace rights, and consider the privileges or disadvantages associated with it, such as fair pay, benefits and opportunities for advancement.
15. **Health:** Consider whether you enjoy good physical and mental health, and reflect on the privileges or disadvantages that come with that, such as access to healthcare and medication, treatment options and overall wellbeing.
16. **Ethnicity:** Reflect on your ethnic or cultural background and consider the privileges or disadvantages associated with it regarding social acceptance, cultural representation and access to resources.
17. **Family, care experienced, caring responsibilities:** Consider whether you have caring responsibilities for children, elderly parents, or other family members, and reflect on the impact it may have on your time, career opportunities and personal wellbeing.
18. **Geographical and travelling amenities:** Reflect on your access to transportation, infrastructure and amenities in your community or country, and consider the privileges or disadvantages associated with it in terms of convenience, opportunities and quality of life.

Remember, whether a privilege is seen as an advantage or disadvantage will depend on the perspective of the individual, the norms of the society that they are part of and where they reside in the world.

Talking about privilege can lead to discomfort. Lean into that feeling and explore why you may feel uncomfortable. This is not about blame. You don't need to apologise for your privileges unless you know you have used them to take advantage of or bully others.

HOW DO WE TEACH CHILDREN AND YOUNG PEOPLE ABOUT PRIVILEGE?

The main themes of this book are social justice and activism. The easiest way to introduce these concepts is by discussing something we can all agree on. The world is full of problems, but caring for our planet is one of the biggest areas that can unite us. We have enough evidence to prove that we must look after our planet.

We are all part of the same planet. Therefore, teaching children about privileges through a focus on environmental privileges is an effective way of starting a discussion about social justice and activism. A more comprehensive discussion around this relates to global citizenship. Our children and young people originate from different parts of the world and when we talk to each other and share our experiences, we gain a better understanding of one another.

Global citizenship is a concept that refers to the rights and responsibilities that individuals have beyond their national borders. We are all part of a larger global community. It is important to teach our children this from a young age so that they understand that we have a shared responsibility for our actions and their impact on others, both locally and globally. When individuals are aware of their privilege, they can use it as a tool for positive change on a global scale.

Our shared privilege is that we live in an area of *environmental advantage*. This term refers to the benefits that the environment provides to humans. If, like me, you live in the UK, on our part of the planet, we have clean air, fresh water, fertile soil and natural resources. This has a positive impact on our health and wellbeing. Exposure to nature and green spaces has been linked to lower levels of stress, improved mood and better academic performance.

When we look at our school environment, it has to be clean and safe by law. We are all responsible for keeping our school environment clean and tidy so that it is safe to use. Not everyone has the same environmental privilege as us. For example, some children in other parts of the world may not have access to clean drinking water.

The following list includes other examples of environmental privileges.

1. **Clean air:** Breathing in clean, unpolluted air is a privilege. In some areas, air pollution from factories, cars, or other sources can make the atmosphere less healthy.
2. **Access to green spaces:** Having parks, gardens, or natural areas nearby to enjoy nature is an environmental privilege. Not everyone has easy access to such green spaces.
3. **Protection from environmental hazards:** Living in an area less prone to natural disasters like floods, hurricanes, or wildfires is an environmental privilege. Some regions face more ecological risks than others.

4. **Waste disposal and recycling:** A well-organised system for waste disposal and recycling in your community is a privilege. In some places, waste management may be less efficient, leading to pollution and environmental problems.
5. **Safe and nutritious food:** Access to safe, nutritious, locally grown food is an environmental privilege. Some areas may have limited access to fresh and healthy food options.
6. **Clean and safe energy sources:** Access to clean and reliable energy sources, such as renewable sources, is a privilege. Power may be less reliable or generated from polluting sources in some places.
7. **Natural beauty and biodiversity:** Living in an area with diverse wildlife and natural beauty, like mountains, forests, or coastlines, is an environmental privilege. These places are often considered valuable for their ecological richness.
8. **Access to public transport:** Having efficient public transportation options can be a privilege, as it reduces the reliance on personal cars, contributing to pollution and traffic congestion.
9. **Protection of ecosystems:** Living in areas where ecosystems are preserved and protected is a privilege. Some regions face challenges like deforestation or habitat destruction.
10. **Clean and safe water:** Access to clean rivers, lakes and oceans for recreational purposes and as a source of livelihood is an environmental privilege. Pollution can threaten these water sources.

Understanding and discussing these examples helps children to recognise that not everyone enjoys the same environmental advantages and that we should work together to protect the environment and ensure these privileges are available to everyone.

PAUSE FOR SELF-REFLECTION

Keeping in our mind our everyday privileges, consider the ways we are all responsible for our school environment.

How might we expand this to think about wider global issues and shared responsibilities as global citizens?

LESSON OR CLASSROOM ACTIVITIES

The following activities provide opportunities for children to learn about privilege. First, through common everyday examples that highlight the ways in which people can be fortunate; then, through an activity that supports children to appreciate privilege and fosters a sense of community and responsibility.

ACTIVITY

TEACHING CHILDREN ABOUT PRIVILEGE THROUGH COMMON EVERYDAY EXAMPLES

OBJECTIVE

It can be easy to take our privileges for granted. We're so used to things we have easy access to we don't always realise how fortunate we are to have them. A good example of this is clean drinking water. We turn on a tap and clean drinkable water comes out. It is fully available in our houses; we don't have to go anywhere to access it. Our right to clean drinkable water is protected by law and there are fines issued to water providers if they don't ensure that our water is clean and safe to drink. In this activity we will use clean drinking water as an example of a privilege that not everyone around the world has.

Introduce this activity to your pupils like this:

> Imagine you're thirsty, like after playing outside on a hot day. You feel that dry feeling in your mouth and want a drink. Now, think about how easy it is to get a cup of clean water from the tap or a bottle. That's because you have a special privilege called 'access to clean water'.
>
> But not all children around the world are as lucky. Some of them don't have clean water to drink. They might have to walk a long way to find water and, even then, the water might not be safe to drink.

So, it's like having an easy advantage or privilege when you can quickly quench your thirst with clean water. It's important to remember that not everyone has this privilege, and we should be grateful for it. We should also try to use water wisely and not waste it so there's enough for everyone, everywhere.

By drawing these parallels, children can understand that their privileges and abilities can be used not only for keeping their surroundings clean but also for being allies and making a positive difference when they witness injustice or discrimination. It encourages them to be proactive and supportive in various aspects of their lives.

INSTRUCTIONS

Ask the children to write down the steps they go through to get water when thirsty. When they have finished, compare what they have said/written with their classmates.

1. **Recognise thirst:** First, you become aware of your body's need for hydration when you feel thirsty.
2. **Locate a source:** Find a suitable source of liquid. This could be a water tap, a water bottle, a glass, or any available beverage.
3. **Access the container:** If using a bottle or a glass, open it or remove the cap or lid to access the liquid.
4. **Pour or fill:** Pour the liquid into a glass or drink directly from the container, depending on your preference and the type of beverage.
5. **Consume:** Take small sips or drink the liquid until your thirst is quenched. Avoid drinking too quickly to prevent discomfort.
6. **Close container lid:** If you've taken liquid from a container, securely replace the cap or lid when done.
7. **Dispose or rinse:** Properly dispose of any leftover liquid or rinse the container for reuse.
8. **Hydrate adequately:** Remember to drink enough to satisfy your thirst and stay hydrated.

ACTIVITY

CLEANING UP OUR LOCAL PARK/GREEN SPACE

OBJECTIVE

How can we demonstrate our appreciation and privilege of being able to access a well-maintained park by taking responsibility for its upkeep? This activity helps improve the local park/green space and fosters a sense of community and responsibility for our environment, using our privileges to benefit the broader community.

INSTRUCTIONS

- Plan a trip to a local park.
- Write a plan around how you could use your privileges for good when you get to the park
- Thinking about your local park/green spaces, answer the following questions using the five Ws (who, what, where, when, why and how) to prompt your answers.
- First, describe your local park/green space.
- *Sentence starter*: Our local park/green space is...

  1. Where is it?
  2. What makes it special?
  3. What activities can you do there?
  4. Think about a happy memory of a time you spent there.
  5. How did that make you feel?
  6. Is it well looked after?
  7. How is it maintained?
  8. Who maintains it?
  9. What can you do to help keep it clean?

- *Sentence starter*: However, there are times when it is neglected ...

  1. How is it neglected?
  2. What are the consequences of this?

3. How does it make you feel when you can see that people don't respect the space?
4. What can you do to help?

- Discuss the list of privileges around being able to access a clean green space.

1. *Resources*: We have time, energy and tools (like bags and gloves) to help clean the park.
2. *Education*: We know many things, like why it's essential to keep the park clean and how to talk to others about it.
3. *Our community*: We have local people who can help us clean the park and spread the word about keeping it clean.
4. *Access to and sharing of information*: We can use a computer to find out about the park, why it is essential and help us find ways to clean it up.
5. *Being a good example*: When we work together to keep the park clean other people will see we are doing good things to help our community. Other people might want to help, too, and younger children will look up to us.
6. *Asking for help*: Sometimes, grown-ups who make rules can help by ensuring the park stays nice and clean. They can remind community members and children that cleaning the park is essential.

REFLECTIVE QUESTIONS

- What is privilege?
- What privileges do we have?
- What privileges did we use to help clean up the park/green space?
- How can we use our privileges to help look after our planet?
- How can we use our privileges to be global citizens?
- How can we use our privileges to help other people?

EXTENDED ACTIVITY

Find out about an environmental activist and write some research about them. Compile these into a class book. Start by reading this excerpt from *Nature Allies: Eight Conservationists Who Changed Our World* by Larry A. Nielson.

> It's easy to feel small and powerless in the face of significant environmental challenges. When climate change forces species to fight for their survival and the planet's last places of wilderness are growing smaller and smaller, what can a single person do? But environmentalism's most incredible change-makers started out living ordinary lives. In *Nature's Allies*, Larry Nielsen uses the inspiring stories of conservation pioneers to show that we can each make a difference through passion and perseverance.
>
> In [these biographies], we meet individuals with little in common except that they all made a lasting mark on our world. Some famous and some little-known to readers, they all spoke out to protect wilderness, wildlife, fisheries, rainforests, and wetlands. They exposed polluting practices and fought for social justice ... *Nature's Allies* pays tribute to them all as it seeks to rally a new generation of conservationists to follow in their footsteps.
>
> (Nielson, 2018, book jacket)

The remarks of Larry A. Nielson remind us that every one of us has the ability to leave a lasting impression through activism. The examples we have focused on are from environmental activists who have encouraged a new generation of conservationists.

How will you be inspired by their stories to be a trailblazer?

REFLECTION

In this section, we have looked at privilege and global citizenship. In the same way that you can be a friend to the environment by keeping it clean and safe, you can also be a friend in the moment to people who might need your support when things aren't fair.

You can call yourselves 'environment protectors'. Just like protectors watch over and care for something precious, you can watch over and care for the environment, ensuring it stays clean and safe for everyone. By organising clean-up activities, we demonstrate how we can positively impact our environment. We can also advocate for better park maintenance and educate others about keeping public spaces clean.

We have learnt that not only are we privileged around the environment we have, like green spaces and parks, we also have personal privileges that help us to do good for our local parks/green spaces.

As well as being an environment protector, like superheroes save the day, you can save the environment by keeping it clean, using resources wisely and standing up for what's right. Every small action you take to protect the environment makes a big difference.

Imagine seeing someone being treated unfairly or the environment getting hurt, like when people litter in a park.

How do we show allyship by our actions?

Our personal privileges related to making sure our local park is clean also help us to make sure we are aware of global challenges related to our environment. I hope this activity has reminded you that you are part of a worldwide community and how important that is.

Being a global citizen is about stepping in to help and make our environment better. Remember, being kind to others, standing up for what's right and working together is also what being a global citizen is all about.

CONCLUSION

In this chapter, we have introduced the concepts of privileges and what our personal privileges are. We then looked at how to analyse and reflect on our own individual privileges and how we may have used them to our advantage.

We considered global citizenship and how we can use our shared concern for the planet to take better care of our environment. We did an activity around looking after our local green spaces that helped us to learn about environmental activism and people who worked hard to raise awareness of environmental issues.

The following section will examine allyship, an essential part of global citizenship.

FURTHER READING AND RESOURCES

FOR ADULTS

Deep Learning for Social Justice by the Schools, Students and Teachers network (SAAT)

Fighting for Deep Social Justice by SAAT
Global Citizenship: The Handbook for Primary Teaching by Ian Davies and Garth Stahl
Teaching for Global Citizenship: A Guide for Schools by David Hicks
Global Citizenship Education: Everyday Transcendence by William Gaudelli

FOR CHILDREN

I'm a Global Citizen: We're All Equal by Georgia Amson-Bradshaw, illustrated by David Broadbent
Be Green! Mindful Kids: Global Citizen by Mandy Archer, illustrated by Katie Abey
Be Kind! Mindful Kids: Global Citizen by Stephanie Clarkson, illustrated by Katie Abey
Growing Good by Bernard Ashley, illustrated by Anne Wilson
Be Kind by Pat Zietlow Miller, illustrated by Jen Hill
Here We Are: Notes for Living on Planet Earth by Oliver Jeffers

2

WHAT IS AN ALLY? WHY IS IT IMPORTANT TO TEACH CHILDREN TO BE INFLUENTIAL ALLIES?

KEY CONCEPTS

The key concepts covered in this chapter are:

What is an ally?

- Someone who speaks out and stands up against discrimination, racism, sexism, homophobia and other forms of oppression.
- Allies are not perfect; they learn as they grow, but they are committed to learning about and fighting against social injustice.

INTRODUCTION

In the last chapter, we learnt about *global citizenship* and how you have the privilege to help look after the environment and other people. In this chapter, we will learn about allyship and teach children how important it is to be a friend to someone when they need one, even if they are not usually friends with them.

WHAT IS ALLYSHIP?

Being an ally means being there for someone when they need it most, even if they are not exactly like us or if we didn't know them before. It means showing care and understanding to people struggling or facing unfair treatment. When we speak to children about what allyship means and how to demonstrate it, we can describe it as 'someone who is a friend in that moment when you need one'.

Using the environment example in Chapter 1, children and young people can understand that we must care for our environment. This example is meant to be simple and easily relatable so that we can help children better understand how allyship applies to various aspects of their lives, including their role as protectors of the environment. Being a good ally to the environment means standing up to protect it and helping others to see the right way to look after it, just like being a good friend.

Next, if we shift the focus from environmental activism to social justice, we can teach examples of how people have stood up for what's right by showing kindness and compassion to others.

WHY IS THIS IMPORTANT?

As adults, we need to model positive behaviour for children and young people. How are children who struggle with their behaviour meant to know what positive behaviour looks like unless we show them? It's the same with modelling allyship. This means speaking out against discrimination when we see it, standing up for others who are being mistreated and working to make our communities more inclusive for everyone.

HOW TO BE A GOOD ALLY?

I would encourage you to read *The Good Ally* by Nova Reid to learn about allyship. The book encourages readers to challenge their beliefs and actively engage in the work of allyship. In the book, Nova Reid explains that being a good ally is about actively listening to marginalised voices, educating oneself, challenging our own biases, amplifying underrepresented voices and taking meaningful action to dismantle systemic oppression and promote equality and justice.

PERFORMATIVE ALLYSHIP

We can't talk about allyship without talking about true allyship in comparison to performative allyship. True allyship involves actively listening, learning and taking meaningful steps to support and uplift people. This consists of a commitment to long-term change. Unfortunately, we have seen lots of people confess to being allies without actively being willing to listen and do the work. My social media timelines are full of people making public declarations of support, understanding and allyship.

The same people then often message me privately to offer empathy, but that's as far as it goes, no real action follows. When needed to show up, they then choose to stay silent to protect themselves. I get it; people are scared of consequences, but when you are a victim of discrimination your choices are more limited. Staying silent has a direct effect on your wellbeing while speaking out can lead to more discrimination.

We saw this with the rise of the Black Lives Matter movement after the public outcry following the murder of George Floyd. Public media posts, black squares and #antiracist hashtags popped up, but without concrete actions to create positive lasting change.

PAUSE FOR SELF-REFLECTION

To make sure that your allyship is not performative, start by:

- *educating yourself* so that we have a deeper understanding of the issues being called out;
- *listening and learning*: truly engaging with individuals and communities, not just as a 'listening exercise' for your gain without any follow-up or commitment – as Maya Angelou famously said, 'when you know better, do better' (Angelou, 2014);
- *setting clear goals*: doing better when you know better means following up by setting clear, measurable and achievable goals.

How will you be part of the change we need to see?

HOW DO WE MODEL GOOD ALLYSHIP?

Having clear objectives will help you stay focused and track progress.

- *Build relationships*: with people who don't look like you or share your privileges. Do this through network and support. Social media is an excellent space for building connections with people with diverse perspectives and lived experiences outside your usual sphere.

- *Advocate*: when you've taken these foundational steps, you're ready to advocate. It involves publicly using your voice and platform to raise awareness about critical issues that affect marginalised groups.
- *Take action*: 'Speak up. Stand up and speak out'. Turn your awareness and knowledge into concrete actions. What can you do? What steps will stretch you outside your comfort zone? Lean into that; that's the space in which you grow. This might involve volunteering, donating to relevant organisations, or organising events or campaigns. You may be worried you will lose friends and acquaintances at this stage. But this is the part where you can distinguish between the two.
- *Campaigning for change*: support policy and legislation changes at a local, regional and national level that align with the goals you have set yourself. Don't be a frequent campaign switcher unless you know a campaign you supported doesn't align with your values.
- *Regularly revisiting your goals*: what has been the impact of your actions? Are you making progress? If not, why not? How will you realign your goals and values? How will you reflect and adapt to your strategies? Are you open to constructive criticism of your actions without being offended and focusing on your feelings first?
- *Stay committed*: we teach our children that growth is long term. We would not expect our children to be ready for the world at the end of primary school. They still have a long journey and will continuously adapt and change as they experience and navigate new challenges. If we give our children this grace, why do we find it hard to apply that to ourselves? Creating positive change is a long and challenging process. It's hard! But it's essential to stay committed, even when faced with obstacles or setbacks.

BE THE CHANGE YOU WANT TO SEE

Be a role model for the change you want to see. Your actions and behaviours will inspire others to get involved.

However, creating concrete, positive change is not about quick fixes. It requires persistence, patience and long-term commitment. We must make a sustained effort to make a meaningful impact on the issues that matter to us.

PAUSE FOR SELF-REFLECTION

Think of a situation in which someone acted as an ally for you.

1. What was the situation you were facing at that time?
2. How did this person support you?
3. How did their support make you feel?
4. What lasting effect did their support have on you?
5. How did their support encourage you to do better?

REFLECTION

As educators, we spend a lot of time, particularly in primary, teaching children what friendship skills are. We teach them what being a good friend is, but do we spend enough time teaching our students what being a good ally is?

- Kindness, compassion and care; being an ally means standing up for someone being treated unfairly or discriminated against.
- It means being a friend to someone who needs one.
- It means being kind and respectful to everyone, even if they are different from you or your usual friends.
- Being an ally is important because it helps make the world a better place.
- When we stand up for others, we help create a world where everyone is treated with respect and kindness.
- To be a true ally means that we have to 'Speak up. Stand up and speak out.'

HOW DO WE TEACH CHILDREN ABOUT ALLYSHIP?

Storytelling is a powerful way to demonstrate the behaviours we want to see. It allows us to connect emotionally, engage our audience and provide concrete examples that inspire action and understanding.

The stories we will learn demonstrate that allyship means being a caring friend in the moment when we're needed, taking action to help others and not just standing by when something is wrong. Like the characters in the story, we must be kind and supportive to others around us and stand up against unfairness or unkind behaviour. However, it is also important to explain how being an ally to someone means being aware of what they express that they need and listen to what they are asking for, not just what we think they need.

Start with the following:

- Do you know what the word 'ally' means?
- When have you heard it before?
- In what ways is being an ally like being a friend?

We have learnt that you can be an ally to the environment by helping to protect it. Just because you may not be directly affected by environmental problems in your area, you can still support and work with those who are. Just as we all help each other to keep our shared school environment and our wider local environment clean and safe, you can also help people facing unfair treatment or challenges. This can be about the environment or helping others; allies advocate for 'what's right' and work to make things equally better for everyone, even if they are not in the same situation.

Remember: being kind, standing up for what's right and working together are what being an ally is all about.

TRUE ALLYSHIP, NOT PERFORMATIVE ALLYSHIP

Explain to children that it is important to be a good friend, especially to others who need it. Talking about how to do this will help demonstrate the difference between being a true ally (a friend in the moment who supports and helps other people) and a performative ally (someone who pretends to be a good friend).

If we pretend to support someone, that is *performative allyship*.

If you pretend to be a good friend or helper but don't do the things that help or make a difference, that is performative. It's like saying nice things or acting like you care but not taking action to improve things.

Imagine if you had a friend who was sad because they got hurt, and you said, 'I'm here for you, and I care,' but you didn't try to help them or comfort them. That would be performative allyship. You're just saying nice words but not being a good friend.

Being a true ally means saying you care and doing things to show that you care. It means taking actions that can improve your friend's situation and, sometimes, this may mean putting their needs before yours.

We want to be genuine allies by not just talking the talk but also walking the walk, which means actively doing things to support and help other people when they need it. This is important because not being a true ally is hurtful. Performative allyship causes a lot of hurt, particularly for the person who trusted someone in that moment of need to help them.

To be a true ally, we need to do a few essential things.

1. *Learn and understand*: We learn what matters to our friends. This helps us understand their feelings and experiences better.
2. *Listen and be there*: We listen carefully when our friends talk to us. We don't just listen to look good, but because we genuinely care about what they have to say. It's like what Maya Angelou said, when we know better, we do better.
3. *Set goals*: We make plans to do things that help our friends and make things better. We set clear goals to see our progress against our good intentions.
4. *Make new friends*: We make friends with all kinds of people, not just those like us. This helps us learn from different perspectives and experiences.
5. *Speak up*: Once we've learnt and listened, we use our voices to discuss important issues affecting our friends. We speak up to help make things fair for everyone.
6. *Take action*: We don't stop at just talking. We take action to make a difference. This might mean helping out, giving to good causes, or organising events to show your support. You could start by doing something in school to show your support for a local cause.
7. *Support change*: We also support rules and laws that make things fairer. We don't change our minds constantly unless we learn something new that makes sense and causes us to question our original beliefs.
8. *Keep checking*: We check to see if our actions are improving things. If not, we figure out how to do better and make changes.
9. *Stay committed*: We know that change takes time. We don't give up when things get tough. We keep going because we want to see good things happen.
10. *Be a role model*: Our actions show others how to be good friends and allies. We inspire others to join us in making the world better.

Remember: making a real difference takes time and effort, but it's worth it. We want to be the change we wish to see in the world, and that's something we can all do together.

You're never too young to learn how important that is.

Learning the difference between true allyship and performative allyship helps us become better friends and makes the world kinder and fairer for everyone. Children and young people might think they are too young to make a difference, but every single one of us is part of a bigger movement.

LESSON OR CLASSROOM ACTIVITIES

The following activities provide opportunities for children to learn about allyship. First, through the power of storytelling; then, through an activity where children learn about the different between true allyship and performative allyship.

ACTIVITY

ALLYSHIP THROUGH STORYTELLING

OBJECTIVE

- To introduce children to the concept of allyship and explore some examples from familiar literature.
- Using stories to inspire and connect us.

Storytelling is a powerful way to transform abstract concepts into lived experiences that we can relate to more easily. Storytelling helps to foster understanding, empathy and change.

Recap the work around environmental activism in Chapter 1. Explain to your children and young people that being a good ally means that just like how you help the environment, you can also help people when things aren't fair. The core values of allyship are kindness and compassion. Start by sharing a selection of well-known stories around these concepts. There are many examples of these from various cultures from all around the world.

Here are some stories to choose from.

THE GOOD SAMARITAN FROM THE BIBLE

Introduction for children: Have you ever heard someone describe someone else as a 'good Samaritan'?

In the story of the good Samaritan, the Samaritan saw someone in need and decided to show kindness and care even though they were different and might not have been friends before.

1. This story is about helping others when they need it. How does it connect to being a good friend and standing up for someone?
2. Imagine you saw someone in trouble but didn't help because you thought someone else would. That's called the bystander effect (something we will learn about later in the book). How could the Good Samaritan story teach us not to let that happen?
3. The Good Samaritan story teaches us to be helpful to people we don't know personally. How can we remember to be helpful and not just watch when we can see that people need us?

4. Can you remember seeing someone who wasn't your friend but needed help? What ideas do you have for being a good helper, like the Good Samaritan, in that situation?
5. If you were in the story of the Good Samaritan, how would you feel if others just walked by? What could you do to ensure you're a caring friend instead of a bystander?

THE SNEETCHES BY DR SEUSS

Introduction for children: A story of two groups of Sneetches, those with stars on their bellies and those without, and how they treat each other with kindness and respect.

1. In *The Sneetches*, some characters with stars on their bellies acted like they were better than others. How do you think the Sneetches who didn't have stars could have been good allies to each other?
2. When the Plain-Belly Sneetches felt left out, some other Sneetches just watched. How could those Sneetches have been better allies and friends to the Plain-Belly Sneetches?
3. Sylvester McMonkey McBean took advantage of the Sneetches' differences to make money. If you were a Sneetch, what could you do to stand up against someone like Sylvester and be an ally to all Sneetches?
4. The Sneetches learnt that having or not having stars didn't make them better or worse. How can we remember this lesson and be allies to people who might be mistreated for something they can't control?
5. At the end of the story, the Sneetches work together to enjoy themselves on the beach. How can we be like those Sneetches, including everyone, being good allies and not leaving anyone out?

THE THREE MUSKETEERS BY ALEXANDRE DUMAS

Introduction for children: The musketeers Athos, Porthos and Aramis stand up for justice and protect each other as loyal allies. The story showcases the importance of being there for one another.

1. In *The Three Musketeers*, how do the main characters help and support each other when they face challenges? Can you think of times when friends or classmates can be allies like this?

2. Sometimes, in the story, people stand by and don't help when something unfair happens. How can we ensure we don't do that in real life and be good allies to those who need it?
3. The musketeers are known for their loyalty and friendship. How can you show loyalty and be a good friend to someone who might be having a hard time?
4. D'Artagnan makes friends with the musketeers and stands up against those who try to hurt them. How can we be brave like D'Artagnan and protect our friends from those who might want to harm them?
5. The musketeers work together to solve problems. Can you think of a time when you helped someone else solve a problem or stood up for them? How did it feel to be an ally?

ALADDIN

Introduction for children: The main characters' choices and interactions with others offer valuable lessons about the significance of standing up for ourselves, helping others and making the right choices that can shape our destiny.

1. At the beginning of the story, the market stallholder mistreats Aladdin. What could other people have done to be allies to Aladdin and stand up against the unfair treatment he received?
2. Sometimes, in the story, characters like the Sultan don't know about Aladdin and Jasmine's difficulties. How can we make sure we're aware of our friends' problems and be good allies to them?
3. In the story, some characters, like the palace guards, follow Jafar's orders even though they know they are wrong. How can we be different and not follow someone when they're doing something terrible?
4. Genie became a true friend and ally to Aladdin. How can we learn from Genie and be the kind of friend who helps, supports and stands up for our friends when they need it?
5. Genie was powerful, but he needed someone to free him. How does this show that sometimes being an ally means helping someone achieve their dreams over our own?

NEXT STEPS

Discuss the story you have chosen to focus on and what the story means to you. Give your students time to create short stories around allyship and showing kindness.

In pairs, ask your students to read their stories with each other and ask questions based on the five Ws:

Who?

What does the story teach us about allies and allyship?

Where?

When?

Why?

ACTIVITY

SPOT THE REAL ALLY

OBJECTIVE

To teach children the difference between true allyship and performative allyship.

MATERIALS NEEDED

- Paper
- Markers or coloured pencils
- Pictures or descriptions of different scenarios

INSTRUCTIONS

1. *Introduction* (5 minutes): Explain to the children what performative allyship is in simple terms. You can use an example of someone pretending to be a good friend but not really doing a lot to help.
2. *Discussion* (10 minutes): Discuss with the children why it's essential to be true allies and not just pretend. Ask them how they feel when someone pretends to be their friend but doesn't help when they really need them to.
3. *Activity* (20 minutes): Divide the children into small groups and provide each group with a scenario involving different actions. These scenarios should represent either true allyship or performative allyship.

For example:

- *Scenario 1*: A friend sees another friend being bullied and stands up to help them.
- *Scenario 2*: A friend sees another friend being bullied but does nothing and walks away.
- *Scenario 3*: A friend posts a message on social media about supporting a cause but doesn't do anything else.
- *Scenario 4*: A friend helps another friend with their schoolwork when they're struggling.

Ask each group to discuss each plan and decide whether it represents true or performative allyship. They could draw a picture, write a short scenario description or record a voice note to explain their decision.

4. *Presentation* (20 minutes): Ask each group to present their scenarios to the whole group. Have them explain why they think it represents true allyship or performative allyship.
5. *Whole-class discussion* (10 minutes): After each presentation, discuss why they made their choices. Encourage the children to share their thoughts on how they can be true allies in real life.
6. *Activity conclusion* (5 minutes): Summarise the key points from the activity and emphasise the importance of being true allies who take action to help others. Ask the children how they will continue learning from today in other situations, such as in the playground, at home and in their local community. Explain that this activity will help them understand the concept of performative allyship and why it's essential to be genuine allies who make a positive impact in the lives of others. Explain that learning begins in the classroom but needs to be extended beyond that and applied to real-life situations for it to stick.

CONCLUSION

In this chapter we have seen the power that storytelling can have and how it helps us to understand challenging concepts. It has also reminded us of historical examples of true allyship from around the world that we can all relate to. We learnt that a true and good ally is someone who is there for an individual when they need them. This is not necessarily someone they know. An ally supports someone in their moment of need, even if they're not connected, such as not being from the same racial background as us or not being part of our usual circle of friends. It means caring about and understanding people who might be going through tough times or facing unfair treatment. It would be good to monitor the lasting impact of the stories and how they have helped your students to remember what being a true ally means. Every so often you may need to remind them of the stories and what they have learnt from them.

FURTHER READING AND RESOURCES

FOR ADULTS

The Shoulders We Stand On by Preeti Dhillon
Diversity in Schools by Bennie Kara
The Good Ally by Nova Reid
What White People Can Do Next: From Allyship to Coalition by Emma Dabiri
Pride & Progress: Making Schools LGBT+ Inclusive Spaces by Adam Brett and Jo Brassington

FOR YOUNG PEOPLE 14+

Being an Ally Edited by Shakirah Bourne and Dana Alison Levy
Allies: Real Talk about Showing Up, Screwing Up and Trying Again Edited by Shakirah Bourne and Dana Alison Levy

FOR CHILDREN

Little Allies Colouring Book: A Children's Colouring Book About Inclusion, Diversity, and Becoming an Ally by Julie Kratz and Edward Maiello
We All Belong: A Children's Book about Diversity, Race and Empathy by Nathalie Goss, Alex Goss and Goss Castle

3

WHAT IS A BYSTANDER?

KEY CONCEPTS

The key concepts covered in this chapter are:

- the role of the bystander and the bystander effect;
- how the inactions of others can cause our own inactions;
- how social influences impact our behaviour.

INTRODUCTION

In the last chapter, we discussed what it means to be a true ally. We also discussed how harmful it is when people pretend to be allies but aren't sincere. Understanding the difference between *true allyship* and *performative allyship* helps us to navigate harmful situations, including *insincere friendships*, that can cause us to lose trust in people and their intentions.

In this section, we'll go on to look at the concept of *bystanders* and the *bystander effect.*

WHAT IS A BYSTANDER?

A bystander is someone who witnesses an event or situation but does not participate in it. The bystander effect is a social psychological phenomenon where individuals are less likely to help a victim when others are present. It became a popular phrase following the infamous 1964 killing of Kitty Genovese in New York City.

The social psychologists Bibb Latané and John Darley popularised the phrase. Their research found that the greater the number of bystanders, the less likely it is for any one of them to help a person in distress. This is due to the *diffusion of responsibility*, where individuals feel less personal responsibility to act when there are more people around. This is also affected by *social influence*, where individuals monitor the behaviour of those around them to determine how to act. They also found that people are more likely to act in a crisis when there are few or no other witnesses present.

Unfortunately, the bystander effect is a phenomenon that we also see in schools. This is most commonly seen in regard to bullying. In this context, research has shown that when bystanders witness bullying, they may feel that someone else will intervene or that it is not their place to get involved. This can lead to a situation of inaction, where no one intervenes, and the bullying continues. The role of the bystanders is pivotal as the bystander effect can either encourage others to speak up or prevent individuals from intervening in a bullying situation.

WHY IS THIS IMPORTANT?

Bystanders have the potential to make a positive difference in a bullying situation by becoming an *upstander*. This is someone who witnesses what happens and intervenes, interrupts, or speaks up to stop the bullying.

There are many things that bystanders can do to become upstanders, such as questioning the bullying behaviour, using humour to redirect the conversation, intervening as a group, walking with the person being bullied and reaching out privately to check in with the victim.

The Suzy Lamplugh Trust offers *active bystander* training called Stand Up Against Harassment (Suzy Lamplugh Trust, 2022). This is designed to empower people to be active bystanders when they see harassment taking place, without putting their own personal safety at risk. The training focuses on the *5 Ds of Bystander Intervention* (Right To Be, n.d.), which was expanded by Right To Be (formerly Hollaback!) from the original concept of the three Ds of bystander intervention pioneered by Green Dot in 2012. The training raises awareness of harassment, upskilling and empowering bystanders to help defuse situations, discourage harassers and support victims.

HOW DO WE MODEL BYSTANDER INTERVENTION?

It's important to teach our children that adults are expected to intervene if they witness someone in distress; it's important to show that we would act and offer help. You can be an active bystander by intervening in an emergency, against a bully, or during an assault or other crime, but you must ensure your safety.

THE FIVE DS OF BYSTANDER INTERVENTION

The Right To Be, five Ds of bystander intervention, emphasise the following methods.

1. **Distract:** This method involves interrupting the incident of harassment by distracting the harasser. For example, you could pretend to be lost and ask the person being harassed for directions or get in between the person harassing and the person being harassed.
2. **Delegate:** This method involves seeking help from someone else to intervene. For example, you could ask a friend or authority figure to help.
3. **Document:** This method involves recording the incident of harassment. For example, you could take a video or photo of the incident.
4. **Delay:** This method involves waiting until after the incident of harassment has ended to intervene. For example, you could check in with the harassed person after the incident.
5. **Direct:** This method involves confronting the harasser directly. For example, you could tell the harasser that their behaviour is not okay.

Following these steps greatly decreases the chance of you becoming a victim too.

OVERCOMING THE BYSTANDER EFFECT

If we know that people are less likely to intervene when they witness harassment, bullying and crime, we can also hope that the opposite could be true. Researchers have identified several factors that can help people overcome the negative bystander effect and increase the likelihood of moving from bystander to upstander by engaging in helping behaviours.

1. *Witnessing helping behaviour*: According to a study by Studte et al., published in 2019, when we observe other people engaging in prosocial behaviours, in this case donating blood, we are more likely to do the same. Seeing someone doing something kind or helpful makes us more willing to want to help others too.
2. *Being observant*: People often say they didn't act when something was happening because they didn't notice someone needed help until it was too late to intervene. They also worry that people don't really need their help. In one famous experiment called the 'smoky room experiment', conducted in 1968 by Latané and Darley, when other people in the room failed to respond, participants were less likely to respond too, even though the room was filling up with smoke! Failing to respond made the participants assume that they were not in an emergency situation.
3. *Being skilled and knowledgeable*: People frequently do nothing because they are unsure of how to intervene, which is why bystander education is crucial. By getting more training to be prepared for anything, we can feel more secure and, therefore, be more likely to be an upstander. For instance, if we are trained in first aid, we are more likely to assist someone who becomes unwell in public.
4. *Guilt*: Studies have shown that helping behaviours can frequently result from feeling guilty. For example, the concept of 'survivor guilt'. After the 9/11 terrorist attacks, survivors were more motivated to assist others in the wake of the incident. They felt guilty that they had survived while others hadn't.
5. *Having a personal relationship*: According to lots of different research, we are more likely to assist people we know personally, who we are familiar with or who we feel a connection to. We are less likely to help strangers as we feel no direct connection with them. Our brains teach us to think about people that are familiar to us so there may be a benefit in helping as, if they remember us, they can help us in the future. This is a concept called reciprocal altruism.
6. *Seeing others as deserving of help*: People are also more likely to help others if they think that the person truly deserves it. In one classic study by Bryam and Test from 1967, participants were more likely to give money to a stranger if they believed that the individual's wallet had been stolen rather than that the person had spent all their money. We make a judgement of the deservingness behind why someone needs our help. The problem with that is people can often manipulate others which is common

within friendship bullying. But when it comes to strangers, we are more likely to help people unfamiliar to us if they seem to have a legitimate reason for needing money. Helping the homeless is an example of this. Some people are more inclined than others to donate money to the homeless because they empathise with their situation and don't see their circumstances as their own fault.

7. *Feeling good*: 'Birds flying high, sun in the sky, breeze drifting on by ... I'm feeling good!' ('Feeling good', Newly and Bricusse, 1964). Nina Simone was right! When we're in a good mood, we're more likely to be more generous with our time and assistance. This is what's known as the feel-good factor; it leaves us in a good mood. At the same time, being helpful will likely leave us feeling good anyway, so do good to feel good.

REFLECTION

Learning about the bystander effect can cause strong feelings, particularly if you've been a victim yourself or have seen instances in which people failed to act. It's important to give these emotions some thought and, if needed, to seek support. Remember that allyship work is emotionally demanding, and making mental health a priority will help you support our children and young people to the best of your ability. Teachers have a tendency to prioritise their students. We are becoming increasingly aware of the need to support children and young people, but at the same time, we must remember that our wellbeing matters too.

The NHS has some good tips for supporting our own wellbeing. It recommends that if feelings of distress last for two to four weeks or longer, you should consider seeking advice from your GP and other support services. In addition, every school is obligated to provide support for staff. Also, the education charity Education Support provides a free, confidential helpline for all teachers, lecturers and staff in England, Wales and Scotland. It's available all day, every day. Details of this can be found in the Further reading and resources section of this chapter.

HOW DO WE TEACH CHILDREN ABOUT THE BYSTANDER EFFECT?

You can start by saying: imagine you're in a big group of friends playing at the park. If someone falls and gets hurt, everyone might stop and stare. You might think of helping, then hesitate and think, 'Oh, someone else will help them'; but everyone else might be thinking the same thing, so no one ends up helping. You wait and wait, and sometimes, nobody ends up helping because they all think someone else will. That's the *bystander effect*.

Bystanders are people who see something happening but choose not to get involved. Sometimes, they're scared to help or think it's not their problem.

It's important to remember that if you see someone in trouble, it's good to be the one who helps, even if you think others will too. Being a *good ally* means not just standing by and doing nothing.

It's not good to be a bystander, to watch others get hurt and not do anything to help. This is a big problem, especially when it comes to *bullying*.

This is something you may have seen happening in schools. The bystander sees the bullying take place and doesn't do anything to stop it. They might stand and watch. When everyone does that, this is what we call the bystander effect. Seeing lots of people not doing anything to help makes us feel like we shouldn't either. When we're scared or anxious, we might forget that we all have the power to influence the lives of others around us.

Some people will always help others whenever they can. They feel bad when they see someone in trouble, like if a friend trips up on something and falls. They're people who always rush to help without thinking twice because they want to make things better.

Some people might feel a bit scared or unsure. They might think, 'Hmm, maybe someone else will help.' It's like when you're playing a game, and everyone thinks someone else will run for the ball if it gets thrown too far. So, sometimes, no one chases after it. But you know what? It's good to help, when possible, even if you think someone else might help. That way, we can all make the world a kinder place.

If you see someone rushing in to help someone else, that doesn't always mean they're braver than you. They might still feel scared, but they don't let fear stop them from doing the right thing. Some people worry that if they step in when someone is being bullied the bully will turn on them too, but if everyone did that it would never stop.

There are five essential things to remember when something isn't right, or someone needs help. The five Ds can help you be an upstander to people needing your help. They are designed to empower you to stand up for others and yourself. Awareness of them is essential because upstanders make the world a better place for everyone. They can be a helpful way to teach you what to do in an emergency or when you see someone in trouble.

The five Ds stand for:

1. distract,
2. delegate,
3. document,
4. delay,
5. direct.

1. *Distract*: Distracting means doing something to take someone's attention away from a problem or a bad situation. For example, if you see someone teasing or being unkind to another person, you can distract them by saying something like, 'Hey, let's play a game together!' This way, you're helping to stop the unkind behaviour and support the victim.
2. *Delegate*: Delegating means getting help from a trusted adult or someone who can make things better. For instance, if you notice someone getting hurt while playing, you can go to a teacher or a parent/carer nearby and say, 'Can you please help? Someone got hurt, and they need your help.' Doing this lets you get the right person to help in the situation.
3. *Document*: Documenting means taking a picture or writing down what's happening if it's safe; doing so shouldn't endanger you. For example, if you see someone breaking the playground rules, you can tell a grown-up later and show them a picture you took with your parent/carer's permission. This helps adults to understand what happened and how to fix it.
4. *Delay*: This means waiting and watching the situation to see if it improves or worsens. For example, if you see two friends arguing but not hurting each other, you can wait a moment to see if they solve it independently. If it gets worse, then you can step in and help.
5. *Direct*: Directing means talking to the person who needs help or the one causing the problem to make things better. If you see someone looking upset because they've lost something, you can talk to them and say, 'Don't worry, we can look for it together.' By talking directly to them, you're being kind and helpful.

These are the five Ds; they help us know what to do when we want to make things better or help someone when something isn't right. I have only given you a short overview here. You can watch videos online that explain this in more detail.

LESSON OR CLASSROOM ACTIVITIES

The following activities provide opportunities for children to learn about bystanders. The first activity encourages you to use an example of a real-life situation as a starting point for supporting children to think about how bystanders can transform into upstanders. The second activity is an opportunity for children to develop their creativity and storytelling skills while learning about the bystander effect.

ACTIVITY

THE FIVE DS

OBJECTIVE

Write down another example for each one of the Ds.

This could be from a natural or made-up event. If your example is from a real-life situation, be careful not to name anyone or talk about them without their permission. In your example, what would have turned the bystander into an upstander?

ACTIVITY

STORY SEQUENCING: CREATING A PHOTO STORY ABOUT THE BYSTANDER EFFECT

OBJECTIVE

You're going to make your own photo story about the bystander effect. This activity helps children understand the concept of the bystander effect and encourages

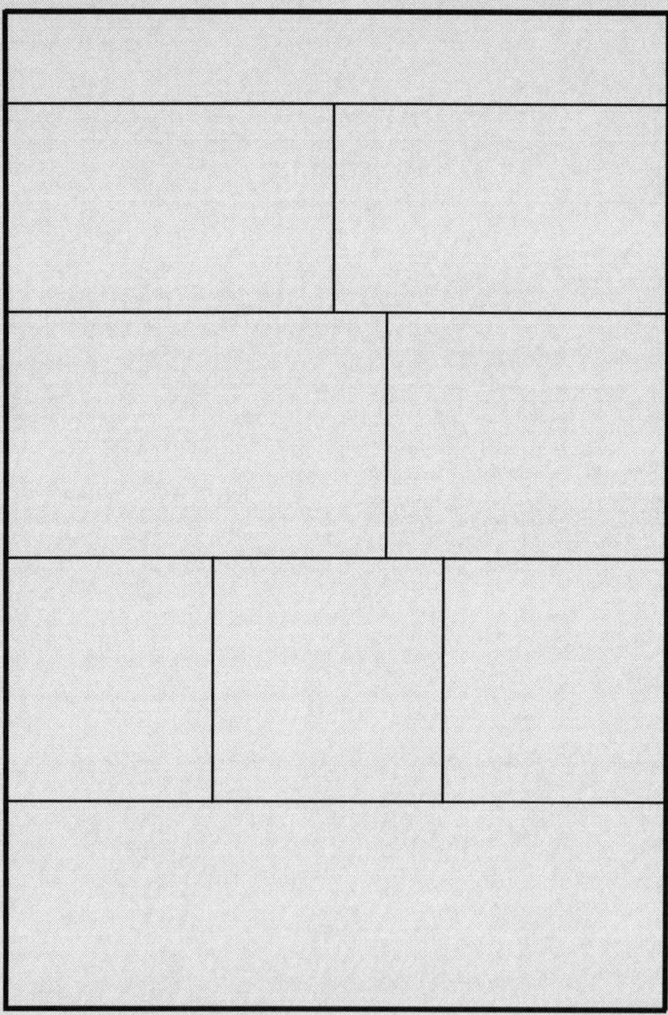

Figure 3.1 Story Sequencing template

creativity and storytelling skills. It also reinforces the idea that being an upstander who helps in such situations is essential to improving the world.

MATERIALS NEEDED

- Paper or notebook
- Pencils
- Scissors
- Old magazines or printed pictures (optional)
- Glue (optional), camera/tablet or smartphone (optional)

Use the template (see Figure 3.1) to help you.

DURATION (1–2 hours)

INSTRUCTIONS

1. *Introduction to the bystander effect*: Begin the activity by explaining the bystander effect to the children simply, using the examples you provided earlier and letting them respond with the examples they thought of. You can say something like, 'The bystander effect happens when people don't help someone in need because they believe others will. We want to create a story about this to help others understand and know what to do if they find themselves in a situation where they might need to use the five Ds.'
2. *Brainstorming*: Ask the children to brainstorm a short story about the bystander effect. Please encourage them to think about a situation where someone needs help, but nobody steps in because they all think someone else will do it. Discuss possible scenarios, like a lost pet, a friend feeling upset because someone is being unkind, or someone getting hurt while playing.
3. *Story outline*: Once they have a basic idea, help the children create an outline of the story. Discuss the beginning, middle and end of the story. What happens first? Who are the characters? How does the situation unfold?
4. *Creating scenes*: Divide the story into critical scenes or moments. Each scene should be a part of the story that can be illustrated with a photo. The children can draw these scenes on separate pieces of paper or use old magazines to cut out pictures that represent the scenes.

5. *Adding captions*: Under each scene or picture, ask the children to write a short caption that explains what's happening in that part of the story. This will help them remember the sequence.
6. *Assembling the story*: Arrange the scenes in the correct order, creating a sequence that tells the story from start to finish. If they're using magazine pictures, they can glue them onto a larger piece of paper appropriately.
7. *Presentation*: Once the photo story is complete, have each child present their story to the group. They can explain the story, its characters and the bystander effect they portrayed in their sequence.
8. *Discussion*: After each presentation, discuss the story and the bystander effect. Ask questions like, 'Why do you think people didn't help in this situation?' or 'What could the characters have done differently?' Try to allow time for everyone to share their thoughts and ideas.
9. *Optional photography*: If you can access cameras, tablets, or smartphones, it would be good to let children take their own photos to illustrate the story instead of drawing or using magazine pictures. This will help them remember that taking photos is a great way to document an event if faced with a scenario outside school. It would be good to remind them about keeping safe while using their phones and the rules around sharing photos/videos online.
10. *Display*: Once all the stories are completed and discussed, you can display them on a wall or in a shared space to share the vital message about the bystander effect with others. With permission, you could also share what you have been learning with parents/carers and encourage a follow-up discussion at home.

CONCLUSION

Through our discussion and activities related to the bystander effect and being an upstander, we have learnt several key concepts.

The bystander effect: We learnt that the bystander effect is when people don't help someone in need because they assume others will, creating a situation where nobody helps.

We understood that the bystander effect can happen in situations like someone getting hurt, being treated unkindly, or feeling sad and lonely.

Being an upstander: We discovered that being an upstander means being an *everyday hero* by standing up and doing the right thing when we see something wrong or when someone needs help.

We learnt that upstanders can help in various ways, like distracting from unkind behaviour, getting help from a trusted adult, or directly talking to someone who needs assistance.

A good ally: We explored that a good ally supports and stands up for others, especially those facing unfair treatment or discrimination.

We learnt that good allies listen to others, speak up against injustice and help create a safe and inclusive environment for everyone.

We've learnt that the bystander effect can sometimes stop people from helping when they should. Being an upstander means being brave and kind, and it's a meaningful way to make the world a better place. A good ally cares about others, stands up for what's right, and helps those needing support or protection. By being upstanders and good allies, we can contribute to a kinder and fairer world for everyone.

FURTHER READING AND RESOURCES

FOR ADULTS

The Bystander Effect: The Psychology of Courage and How to be Brave by Catherine Sanderson

Why We Act: Turning Bystanders into Moral Rebels by Catherine A. Sanderson

We Are Not Here to Be Bystanders: A Memoir of Love and Resistance by Linda Sarsour

Kitty Genovese: The Murder, the Bystanders, the Crime That Changed America by Kevin Cook

Education Support's free, confidential helpline for all teachers, lecturers and staff in England, Wales and Scotland. Available at: https://www.educationsupport.org.uk/

FOR CHILDREN

Right To Be has developed a range of videos for children on bystander intervention available on YouTube. Available at: https://www.youtube.com/@iHollaback

Stay Strong! Mindful Kids: An Activity Book for Young People Who Are Experiencing Bullying by Sharie Coombes, illustrated by Katie Abey

Bullies, Bigmouths and So-Called Friends by Jenny Alexander

What Is Empathy? A Bullying Storybook for Kids by Amanda Morin

4

CHALLENGING BIAS AND STEREOTYPES

KEY CONCEPTS

The key concepts covered in this chapter are:

- what is bias? Exploring its different forms and how they may show up;
- how do we challenge bias and stereotyping (including our own)?
- what does it mean to treat everyone's children as our own? What are our legal duties around this?

INTRODUCTION

So far, we have looked at the concepts of allyship and, at the same time, what it means to act as a bystander. This chapter will now explain how to challenge bias and stereotypes in everyday situations. We will learn what these concepts mean and how different forms of bias and stereotyping can impact on our lives so that we are better equipped to challenge them.

WHAT IS BIAS?

The term 'bias' has evolved into a concept that has helped raise our awareness of discrimination. We use it to describe unfair or discriminatory attitudes and actions that result in discrimination or unequal treatment towards someone.

Biases are based on stereotypes, whether negative or positive. They are our brain's way of creating shortcuts, which lead to prejudgement.

We know that bias starts in childhood, so it's an important age to unlearn it. The attitudes and beliefs of parents and carers will greatly influence a child's views and perceptions. For example, we all like and dislike certain foods. As the first influence on a child, the culinary preferences of parents/carers will be adopted, which means that children may develop a bias towards those foods. The same applies to hobbies and interests. Children can be influenced by what their parents/carers enjoy. If a parent/carer plays a certain sport, they will likely want their child to play that, too. These examples are generally more of a preference, but they can become harmful when they involve discriminatory or prejudiced views. Children may hear and observe biased opinions, behaviours and beliefs at home, such as gender-biased roles. This can have a negative influence on their interactions with other children.

Hearing bias from loved ones is challenging. Hearing people you care for and respect expressing harmful opinions is confusing. This is bound to create emotional conflict in anyone. It is vital that we, as educators, are mindful of this. Our role is to support our pupils in forming their values and perspectives based on mutual respect and acceptance of differences. To do this, we must ensure that we have been critical of our bias and its effects on how we treat others.

AFFINITY BIAS

Affinity bias refers to the fact that we tend to feel more similarities towards people who have the same characteristics as us, such as race, sexuality and gender, but also more simply in terms of background, hobbies, interests and experiences.

For example, I am an *artist*, I used to be an *art teacher* and my degree is in photo media. I may narrow my connections on social media by searching for people with whom I have shared common interests, such as art and education. However, if I then decided to only promote or repost things from people who share the same interests as me, regardless of what they were talking about, that would be preferential treatment (whether consciously or unconsciously) as I would be giving them more attention, and therefore an advantage, over other people.

In a more harmful way, it is thought that affinity bias can stop us from supporting others because our natural tendency is to favour people similar to us. This can prevent us from showing empathy if others do not conform to our groups. Generally, when we find it harder to challenge discrimination or injustice against people not members of similar groups (because they do not share our protected characteristics), this is affinity bias.

UNCONSCIOUS BIAS

Unconscious bias, by its very definition, refers to biases or prejudices that individuals may hold without being aware of them. We know that these biases are automatic and can influence our judgements and actions without conscious intention and that we all have them. However, when harmful biases are not actively addressed, they become conscious. These are deliberate actions through thoughts, words and actions. Claiming unawareness of our bias should not be used as an excuse to avoid self-reflection, re-education and taking action to stop discrimination, especially when we are made aware of our biases. It's important for us as educators to reflect and not justify harmful behaviour by saying that an individual was unaware of their bias. Whether you agree or not that a discriminatory action is due to conscious bias, the victim of discrimination should not be burdened with proving that discrimination has occurred before action is taken.

Although I may not initially be aware of unconscious bias, it should be argued that if I don't change what I'm doing once my bias is brought to my attention, that it becomes conscious bias.

CHALLENGING STEREOTYPES

Bias can fuel stereotypes that lead to discriminatory behaviour because they make us form unfair generalisations of people. Stereotypes are oversimplified, frequently prejudiced assumptions or ideas that people have about a specific group or category of people. These opinions might not fairly reflect the range and complexity of people within that group since they may be based on traits like age, nationality, gender, or colour.

Loota Rajalin, a Swedish educator and supporter of inclusive and gender-neutral education in Swedish pre-schools, is among the most well-known individuals to have confronted prejudices in the field of education. She is recognised for her work to undermine and lessen gender stereotypes in early childhood education. Her career started in *Nicolaigarden*, a Stockholm pre-school. She noticed that children were being unfair towards one another based on their stereotypes around gender roles.

Rajalin's strategy for promoting gender-neutral education centred on lessening the impact of gender stereotypes in areas including play, clothing and behaviour. Her goal was to establish a space where her students could express themselves and make decisions based more on their interests than what society normalised as the right way for genders to be.

As a result of the environment that was created in this pre-school, other educators used it as a model for inclusive education where children could make decisions based on their interests rather than cultural expectations.

IN LOCO PARENTIS

In recent years, there has been a lot of debate in education around the views of educators as opposed to those of parents/carers, with many people falsely stating that schools are teaching pupils concepts around gender-neutral ideas without the knowledge or consent of parents/carers. As educators, it is important to respect students' preferred gender identities. We can't say we are committed to creating inclusive and respectful learning environments if we don't model this ourselves.

As a headteacher in a special school, I often had pupils who were questioning their identity and identified as non-binary. There was never a time that this wasn't discussed with parents/carers, but this was always with the child's consent. I was never in a situation where a pupil did not want us to talk to parents/carers about their choices; their parents/carers often instigated these discussions, but this fact differs from the narrative pushed in the media.

Fundamentally, for me, our job as educators is to ensure that all our pupils feel safe, respected and belong in our school communities.

The term 'in loco parentis' refers to the legal responsibility of schools and teachers to act in the best interests of their students, as if they were the students' parents. Schools and teachers must provide students with a safe and secure environment, promote their welfare and ensure a good education. Legally, while not bound by parental responsibility, teachers must behave as any reasonable parent would in promoting a child's welfare and ensuring their safety while in their care.

Read and reflect on the following sentences.

I don't know what it is about them; I just can't stand that child.

He's just so arrogant.

She ruins my lessons every time.

Thank God they're not in today; they are so annoying.

They need to be excluded; we'd all be better off without them.

If you don't care about certain students, how can you act in the place of parents and carers?

Teacher bias can hinder our ability to act *in loco parentis* effectively. When biases exist, it will lead to unequal treatment of students, affecting their well-being and development. We might think they can't see it, or you hide the fact that you don't like them, but they know. The most important lesson I have learnt from working in alternative provision, especially with children permanently excluded from mainstream schools, is that relationships matter. We can't fulfil our role *in loco parentis* and provide consistent care, guidance and support if we don't show care and respect for every one of our students, especially those who seem to do their best to push us away.

CHILD Q

Addressing bias is essential to ensure that our education system is equitable and inclusive for all our students. Moreover, we need to take an active role to ensure it is.

One incident that showed that educators were not acting *in loco parentis* is the case of Child Q (BBC News, 2022). Child Q was subjected to a strip search by police officers in school. Instead of acting like parents, the school failed to protect her. They allowed the search without any other adult's presence and did not even inform her parents/carers. The school failed in its duty of care to protect her. As a mother to Black children, this incident raised a deeper question for me. Does society view Black children as everyone's children? The fact that Child Q, a Black girl, endured this ordeal without the support and supervision that should be extended to any child reveals a deeply troubling issue for me. We must ensure that all children are treated with the same level of care as our children and those within our families.

Don't all our children deserve the same care and protection in our society? Safeguarding is a collective responsibility.

HOW DOES BIAS SHOW UP IN TEACHERS?

Educators, like any other individuals, can be biased. And, like any individual, this can be implicit or explicit. An essential part of working within diversity, equality and inclusion (DEI) is raising our self-awareness by examining our biases and prejudices. We must recognise that, like everyone, we may have biases that can inadvertently affect our teaching and student interactions. For example, we all have preconceived notions, prejudices and stereotypes about our preferred teaching styles. This may affect our interactions with students and how we respond to their learning needs.

Fundamentally, students thrive when their basic needs are met, nurtured, supported, cared for and respected. As educators, it is important to remember this, notice when stereotypes arise and challenge ourselves over these. Question yourself regularly, listen without being defensive and take action if your bias is pointed out to you.

ASSESSMENT

There is a long history of bias in assessments, particularly intelligence testing of marginalised groups. A lot of my work is around intersectionality between race and special educational needs and disabilities (SEND) based on the fact that Black Caribbean boys in particular are less likely to be assessed as 'more able', less likely to have their additional needs accurately assessed and more likely to be permanently excluded from education. In October 2023, the House of Commons produced a research briefing titled *Educational Outcomes of Black Pupils and Students* (Roberts and Bolton, 2023) which focused on this topic. With a specific focus on students in England, this briefing examines the GCSE educational outcomes for Black school students, as well as their progression into further education and the workforce. There are many reasons for the underachievement of Black Caribbean boys in particular. We know that teacher bias starts from a young age, particularly through question phrasing, cultural language preferences and stereotypes. Additionally, bias stems from the use of complex language that can disadvantage certain students, particularly those with undiagnosed speech, language and communication needs (SLCN). Lack of diversity in teaching materials, curriculum content that doesn't meet the needs of all students, and low teacher expectations can compound these issues further. This is why screening assessments for bias before they are used on a large scale is so important.

In an article for *Tes Magazine* by Gráinne Hallahan, published in September 2021, the author talks about what they describe as the 'assessment bias trap' and what the teacher-assessed grades (TAGs) that were used during the 2020–1 academic year (during the pandemic when students could not physically sit exams) have taught us about assessment bias. Hallahan states, 'Every assessment a school conducts is at risk of unconscious bias ... It's not a criticism of teachers, but rather an inherent part of human judgement' (Hallahan, 2021).

Teachers were expected to create, administer, mark and then award grades with full knowledge of who each student was, which rightly raised concerns about the risk of teacher bias. This resulted in a review of research into bias by Ofqual (Newton, 2021), which 'highlights the importance of having safeguards in place, including quality assurance arrangements'.

BEHAVIOUR MANAGEMENT

According to Ofsted, managing poor behaviour in the classroom is one of the main causes of low morale among teachers (Ofsted and Spielman, 2019). Bias can also affect how we handle behaviour in the classroom. Sometimes, we may have different expectations for students based on their background and cultural assumptions that can lead to us reacting differently to the same behaviours being displayed by members of different cultural groups to our own. We might see a certain group of students as too loud or disruptive. We might give other students harsher punishments or, the opposite, be more lenient as we fear they may be subject to harsher treatment at home. We see this in the disproportionate exclusion rates between boys and girls, and certain ethnic minority groups such as Gypsy Roma traveller (GRT) and Black Caribbean boys, who currently have the highest rate of exclusions from mainstream schools, as published in the Department of Education annual figures (DfE, 2023a).

An increasing number of schools are seeing the benefits of using *restorative justice* methods (focusing on repairing the potential harm caused by behaviour rather than simply punishing the behaviour), which encourages accountability and empathy, allowing students to learn from their mistakes and understand the impact of their actions.

At the same time, *reparative justice* emphasises making amends for behaviour that affects others, often through actions that benefit the whole school community. This approach can help students develop a sense of responsibility, belonging and community engagement.

Both approaches encourage growth and understanding rather than fostering resentment or misunderstanding. The whole point of both approaches is to ensure that your school environment is somewhere where everyone feels heard, understood and respected. I have found that this approach is particularly important for neurodivergence (such as autism, ADHD, dyslexia and dyspraxia, as well as generalised anxiety), where it is important that rules are clear, fair and justifiable and cannot be misinterpreted. Most importantly, restorative justice and reparative justice methods prioritise understanding the underlying causes of behaviours rather than punishment.

Respect works both ways, so unless we are prepared to have open, constructive conversations about behaviour through restorative and reparative justice, we will not be able to foster greater understanding and respect between students and teachers.

CLASS PARTICIPATION

A learning environment's dynamics can be impacted by bias in class participation in a number of ways. As teachers, we may unintentionally give preference to pupils who share our interests or points of view. This may lead to unequal opportunities, in which certain students inadvertently marginalise particular views by receiving more attention or speaking opportunities than others. Biases based on culture and language might make it difficult for pupils from different backgrounds to conform to specific communication patterns or to overcome language hurdles. Slang and other informal forms of communication may be viewed as inappropriate, and educational institutions may mandate the use of only standard English while speaking and writing.

Another factor that we know to be present is gender bias, where some students may be given preference or opportunity based on the gender assigned to them at birth. Boys are more likely to be praised for being intelligent and creative, while teachers tend to focus on praising girls for making an effort and being diligent in their work. At the same time, gender bias can result in the unequal representation of women and girls and the hidden contributions of women and girls in history. Tackling bias in classroom participation requires deliberate efforts to guarantee equitable opportunities for all, to value the diversity of viewpoints and to create an inclusive classroom culture that motivates each student to share their special insights. We must be confident that if gender bias and stereotypes can be reinforced, they can also be challenged (UNESCO and Global Education Monitoring Report Team, 2022).

As teachers we may make assumptions about our students' skills and interests based on our own stereotypes. A study by DeCuir-Gunby and Bindra (2022) looked at how implicit teacher bias and attitudes towards students shaped their impact on students. The authors made the case that prejudice and stereotypes do affect how teachers view their students and how this changes their expectations for their students. It also made clear the necessity for additional research on how to reduce prejudice and promote inclusive and equitable education.

A platform called Teachly claims to do just that. Its developers designed it to 'help educators create a more effective and inclusive classroom' (Teachly, n.d.). This is done by capturing data around which students dominate classroom discussion, then using student profiles to analyse their experiences.

CURRICULUM

When it comes to the subjects studied in schools and which ones get chosen, curriculum bias has a significant effect on what pupils learn and how they view the world. This prejudice can take many different forms, such as underrepresenting particular cultures, viewpoints, or histories, which results in a skewed and incomplete understanding of the world. We know that cultural bias leads to the neglect of important contributions from non-dominant cultures. This is why work around decolonising the curriculum is so important. Calls to decolonise the curriculum have grown louder and louder as educators have a growing understanding of how bias therein can perpetuate stereotypes, reinforce inequalities and marginalise certain groups of students.

PUPIL EXPECTATIONS

Bias in pupil expectations can significantly influence students' educational experiences. When teachers have preconceived notions about a student's abilities, potential, or behaviour based on their background, it can result in differential treatment and opportunities. This bias may lead to lower expectations for some students, limiting their chances for academic success and personal growth. Conversely, higher expectations for certain students can create undue pressure, affecting their wellbeing. Addressing bias in pupil expectations requires educators to examine their assumptions and beliefs, providing equal opportunities and tailored support to every student, regardless of their background, to ensure a fair and nurturing learning environment where all students can thrive.

WHY IS IT IMPORTANT TO BE SELF-AWARE?

This is an important question. We can't state that we are committed to creating respectful and equitable learning environments if we're not prepared to challenge ourselves on our own bias and stereotyping. This is not easy to do but the questions below will give you focus areas to help you reflect and become more self-aware.

PAUSE FOR SELF-REFLECTION

1. *Personal awareness*: Am I aware of my biases and prejudices that might impact my teaching?
2. *Inclusive practices*: How am I actively promoting diversity and inclusion in my classroom?
3. *Student wellbeing*: How do I support students facing discrimination or oppression?
4. *Curriculum and resources*: Does my curriculum include diverse perspectives and histories?
5. *Collaboration and advocacy*: How can I collaborate and advocate for equity within my school?
6. *Feedback and improvement*: Am I seeking and using feedback to improve my inclusivity efforts?
7. *Long-term impact aspiration*: How can I contribute to a more just and inclusive society through my role as an educator?

HOW DO WE MODEL CHALLENGING BIAS?

In the book *The End of Bias: Can We Change Our Minds?* by Jessica Nordell (2022), the author explores the capacity of human minds to change. The book delves into the science and psychology of changing one's beliefs and behaviours, offering insights into the factors that influence these transformations. Nordell discusses real-life examples and research findings that shed light on the dynamics of changing our minds. It highlights how crucial it is to be exposed to various viewpoints and experiences because this can help lessen and combat prejudice.

Education, empathy and open-mindedness have always been crucial for educators. Nordell emphasises the importance of exposure to diverse perspectives and experiences, which can help challenge and mitigate biases. The book also discusses strategies for self-reflection and critical thinking to counteract bias and make more informed, unbiased decisions. Reading this book should help us consider more deeply addressing and reducing biases in our thinking and behaviour.

PAUSE FOR SELF-REFLECTION

Self-reflection is essential for personal growth and recognising biases. There are tests that you can complete online to help you explore your own innate biases, such as the Project Implicit test by Harvard University (Project Implicit, n.d.).

Below are some simple questions you can ask yourself.

- Am I treating all my students equally, regardless of their background or characteristics?
- Do I have preconceived notions about any of my students based on their race, gender, or other factors?
- Are there specific students I find it harder to connect with or understand? Why?
- How do I respond when a student challenges my authority or ideas?
- Have I ever made assumptions about a student's abilities or potential without evidence?
- Do I include diverse perspectives and materials in my teaching?
- Am I aware of my emotional reactions when dealing with different students?
- Have I addressed my biases, such as attending training or seeking feedback?
- Do I try to refer to children by their names rather than their genders?

HOW DO WE TEACH CHILDREN TO CHALLENGE BIAS?

For young children, it is easier to challenge biases that have not yet been deeply ingrained.

Sesame Street, a long-running children's television programme, has been recognised for addressing bias and promoting diversity. The show incorporates valuable lessons on bias through its characters and storylines, aiming to teach children about inclusion and respect for others.

This is done through:

- diverse characters (using a wide range of characters from different backgrounds, races and abilities);
- including storylines that address topics like prejudice, discrimination and stereotyping;
- special guests, such as celebrities and experts, to discuss important issues in a child-friendly manner;
- providing additional resources and materials for parents/carers and educators to facilitate further discussions around the topics covered.

This helps young viewers learn about empathy, respect and the importance of treating all individuals with kindness and fairness.

LESSON OR CLASSROOM ACTIVITIES

Both the following activities aim to foster self-awareness and empathy. The second activity encourages children to think creatively and imaginatively about the diversity of others. In contrast, the first activity focuses on self-reflection and understanding one's identity and biases. These activities provide a well-rounded approach to promoting inclusivity and challenging stereotypes.

ACTIVITY

CHALLENGING STEREOTYPES

OBJECTIVE

The following activity is designed to help you support children in challenging their biases and stereotypes. It helps them self-reflect, celebrate diversity, build empathy and engage with their families and wider communities.

EQUIPMENT NEEDED

- A4 or A3 plain paper
- All about me questions
- Pencil
- Colouring pencils (including different flesh-tone pencils)

INSTRUCTIONS

Ask students to draw a picture of themselves in their favourite outfit and answer the following questions. Ask them to explain why they have chosen their clothes and what they mean to them.

This activity might take children different lengths of time. They don't have to complete all the questions. They are designed for them to feel comfortable and to discover common traits. It would be good to photocopy these and share them with families. The questions can be found in Table 4.1 overleaf.

Table 4.1 Adopted from the student questionnaire (primary version) by Jeanne Tolliday, London Borough of Bexley

Name
What does your name mean?
Where is it from?
Why is it special?
Do you have any pets? Can you tell me about them?
What is your favourite animal? What do you like about that animal?
Who is in your family?
What is your favourite thing to do at home?
What is your favourite TV programme?
What is your favourite food? Is there a special treat you enjoy?
What is your favourite colour?
What is your favourite film?
What do you think you are good at?
What do you like best at school?
What do you like least at school?
What is your favourite book or story? What do you like about it?
Tell me something you are good at in school.
What would your teacher say you are good at?
Who are your friends? What do you like about them?
What would make school better for you?
What job do you want to have when you finish school? What do you think the job will be like?
What would you like to get better at?

ACTIVITY

MY NEW FRIEND

OBJECTIVE

This second activity explores connections we have with friends or would like to have. It involves students creating an outline of a friend and answering questions about that friend (real or imaginary).

INSTRUCTIONS

Pair students up with class members they don't ordinarily regularly interact with or give them an outline of a person. Give students the following questions.

1. What do they look like?
2. Do they identify as he/she or they?
3. What is their cultural background?
4. What is their favourite food?
5. What is their favourite music?
6. What are their favourite activities?
7. Do they find learning hard or have a disability?
8. If you could go on a day out or adventure together, where would you go?
9. What is their favourite hobby/activity to do at home?
10. What is their favourite TV programme?
11. What is their favourite food? Is there a special treat they enjoy?
12. What is their favourite colour?
13. What is their favourite film?
14. What do you think they are good at?
15. What is their favourite book or story? What do you like about it?

Ask them to reflect:

- what have you learnt about them that you didn't know before?
- what do you like about them?

- what does your new friend have in common with you?
- what makes you and your friend different to each other?
- do these differences matter? Why/why not?

Then gather together for a group discussion: reflect on what you've learnt and how it's helped you understand the importance of embracing differences and challenging stereotypes.

CONCLUSION

In this chapter, we looked at different types of bias by explaining the key concepts of affinity bias, unconscious bias, stereotypes and the meaning of *in loco parentis*. We explored how bias can influence our decision making as educators, specifically through assessment, behaviour management, class participation and pupil expectations. We then went on to look at the importance of our self-reflection.

We learnt that changing our minds can change how we see 'the other'. In *The End of Bias: Can We Change Our Minds?*, Jessica Nordell states that individuals can change their bias by 'transforming the minds, hearts, and habits of individuals' (2022, p. 381). This is through better and more positive representation, self-reflection, acknowledging and celebrating differences, challenging norms such as gender stereotypes and increasing one's sense of belonging.

We discussed examples of this, such as the experiments done by Loota Rajalin in Swedish pre-schools and children's programmes such as *Sesame Street*.

In conclusion, we must remember that societal bias and stereotypes have existed for thousands of years, but that doesn't mean they can't be challenged. We must start by reflecting on our preferences if we hope to dismantle structural thinking. The most important thing is committing to change and learning from our mistakes. We have to be mindful of the harm that bias does to others.

FURTHER READING AND RESOURCES

One of the main reasons why I wrote this book was because I couldn't find any appropriate resources for primary education around bias and how to challenge it. There are plenty of articles but not many that are solution-focused in a practical way. I hope this chapter fills this gap. However, the articles below are interesting reads as an overview of the challenges we face in moving towards a solution-focused outcome.

Smith, J., Meyer, F. and McClure, H. (2023) The persistence of bias in education: A call for research to move policy and practice from aspiration to results. *Policy Futures in Education*. https://doi.org/10.1177/14782103231180423

Megalokonomou, R. (2021) Teacher gender bias is real and has lasting effects on students' marks and study choices. *The Conversation*. Available at: https://theconversation.com/teacher-gender-bias-is-real-and-has-lasting-effects-on-students-marks-and-study-choices-171827 (Accessed: December 2023)

National Association for Multicultural Education (NAME) How do I know if my biases affect my teaching? Available at: www.nameorg.org/learn/how_do_i_know_if_my_biases_aff.php (Accessed: December 2023)

5

TACKLING DIFFERENT FORMS OF PREJUDICE, DISCRIMINATION AND OPPRESSION

KEY CONCEPTS

The key concepts covered in this chapter are:

- what prejudice, discrimination and oppression mean;
- how these can manifest;
- our duties as educators;
- supporting children to challenge discriminatory practices (anti-attitudes).

INTRODUCTION

So far in this book we have looked at the concepts of *privilege, allyship* and the *bystander effect*. We have also looked at *bias*, including *affinity bias* and how to challenge *stereotypes*.

We will now go on to look at different forms of *prejudice, discrimination* and *oppression*.

Under the Equality Act 2010, it's illegal to discriminate against someone for any of the following reasons:

- age
- disability

- gender reassignment
- marriage and civil partnership
- pregnancy and maternity
- race
- religion or belief
- sex
- sexual orientation.

These are all protected characteristics under the Equality Act. It could be argued that there should be more, such as protection for people going through the menopause and for those who are care-experienced; however, these are the agreed ones.

WHAT IS PREJUDICE, DISCRIMINATION AND OPPRESSION?

All three terms – 'prejudice', 'discrimination' and 'oppression' – are related to bias and inequality. These ideas frequently collide and negatively support injustice and social inequity. It's always best to make sure we understand the definitions and meanings of these terms ourselves because they might be difficult to explain to children and young people.

So, in the simplest terms,

- prejudice is a set of attitudes;
- discrimination is the actions and behaviour that go along with prejudice;
- oppression is use of power to mistreat particular groups.

Below are more detailed definitions from the *Cambridge English Dictionary*. For each definition, I have added how this relates to our legal system in England.

Prejudice: An unfair and unreasonable opinion or feeling, especially when formed without enough thought or knowledge.

It comes from the Latin 'pre' (before) and judge.

In the legal sense, the word is used as a technical term as an action taken 'with prejudice' or 'without prejudice'. In this sense, a legal action taken with prejudice is final, while 'without prejudice' is used to indicate that material cannot be used as evidence.

Discrimination: Treating a person or particular group of people differently, especially in a worse way than that in which you treat other people. The word also means the ability to see the difference between two things or people.

In the legal sense, discrimination is the unfair treatment of someone because of their protected characteristics, background, or circumstances. It involves actions, policies, or practices that disadvantage or harm certain individuals or groups, often due to prejudice or bias.

Oppression: A situation in which people are governed in an unfair and cruel way and prevented from having opportunities and freedom. It also means a feeling of being uncomfortable and worried.

In the legal sense, oppression can take many forms through societal discrimination and systemically, which can be harder to recognise as it is embedded in our structures. It is harder to challenge in countries where oppression against certain groups, such as women and girls, is legal.

Once again, I have tried to define these as simply as possible because understanding these key terms is crucial as they form the foundation for addressing and combating equality and social justice issues. As educators, we don't always explain these concepts the right way and definitions can change over time. This is why it's so important to keep up to date with current thinking around these. In the 2017 research paper 'Culture, prejudice, racism, and discrimination', the author John Baldwin questions, in the context of racism, whether it is 'an individual phenomenon, or does it refer to an intolerance that is supported by a dominant social structure?' (Baldwin, 2017). This is an interesting question; when we apply it to prejudice, discrimination and oppression, we see that these are perpetuated through individual attitudes and actions as well as systemic frameworks – which also support intolerance.

The next step in our learning is to reflect on the way society as a whole supports intolerance, but also, on a micro level, our role in addressing these issues in the classroom. Regardless of whether we are being supported to do so or not, our primary goal as educators is to create an inclusive and equitable learning environment for all students where everyone is supported from their starting points to thrive, regardless of their backgrounds or characteristics.

HOW DO THESE MANIFEST IN EVERYDAY SITUATIONS?

Have you ever been in a space in which you are meant to feel included, but you still feel excluded? You just don't feel like you belong. Nothing is overtly said or done, it is more subtle, so you can't necessarily prove that you are a victim of discrimination. In fact, people seem shocked or hurt when you try and express your feelings. They get defensive, choosing instead to put someone's behaviour towards you down to misunderstandings, leaving you wondering whether your concerns are wrong. You start to question yourself, which starts to impact your wellbeing and mental health. Then the gaslighting starts, you start to lose your confidence. You still attempt to speak up, then you are told that your actions are the ones that are hurtful to others. You feel like your only choice is to get out. You go from feeling excluded to actually being forced to leave.

Micro-aggressions are subtle, often subconscious behaviours, such as acts or comments, that express negative, unfavourable attitudes or prejudiced beliefs towards a specific group or individual. The term was first used by Dr Chester M. Pierce in the 1970s. He saw that micro-aggressions are commonly based on factors such as race, gender, religion, or other characteristics. They create hostile and unfair environments. These cues can be verbal, non-verbal, or contextual to the environment such as work or school. They include actions such as dismissive gestures, stereotyping and other subtle forms of discriminatory behaviour. It is often the case that because micro-aggressions are often seen as unintentional, the perpetrator is not held to account for their actions. This raises questions around responsibility and accountability. Micro-aggressions are harmful. They reinforce prejudice and create a hostile or unwelcoming environment for those who experience them. Part of being an ally is recognising and responding to micro-aggressions that you witness, especially when they are aimed at other people in a subtle way, making them harder to prove.

In schools, micro-aggressions can be seen through stereotyping, invalidating a student's experiences, making derogatory comments, engaging in cultural appropriation, or even explicit biased behaviour. These micro-aggressions can reinforce stereotypes, marginalise certain students and hinder their educational and emotional development. As educators, it is our role to show all our students that they are welcome in our schools. Recognising and responding to micro-aggressions is critical for fostering a sense of belonging through acceptance.

Micro-aggressions through school policies

Micro-aggressions connected to school and wider educational policies can take many forms, many of which, at their core, are a reflection of wider prejudices in society. Policies concerning hair, for instance, that unjustly single out specific textures or styles encourage prejudice. Restrictions against natural hairstyles among specific ethnic and racial groups, for instance, need to be recognised as micro-aggressions if they imply that the looks are unsuitable or not professional. I have afro hair and I wear it in a variety of natural styles. I am often in schools where they have not seen people with natural afro hair. It is important for me to show children and young people that despite the opinion of some adults, my natural hair is professional. Proactive steps have been taken to counteract micro-aggressions related to hair and bring about change, such as World Afro Hair Day, which was founded in 2017 by Michelle De Leon. It is celebrated on 15 September every year and includes research such as the Hair Equality Report, 'The Big Hair Assembly' for schools and training for workplaces.

Another topical discussion is around uniform. The word itself means 'consistent or identical'. Why do we insist that girls wear skirts and boys wear trousers? Why do we insist on smart businesswear for staff? How do we ensure that uniform and what staff wear is affordable?

At the same time, unintentionally targeting specific cultural or religious practices, gender expressions, or socioeconomic origins can occur when regulations are uniform, too rigid and therefore lack cultural sensitivity or inclusivity.

Another example of how micro-aggressions can be seen at the core of other school policies, is through our exclusion policies. As reported in the *Independent* in 2020, we know that Caribbean boys and Gypsy Roma traveller children, in particular, are more likely to be excluded than any other ethnic groups (Tidman, 2020) This demonstrates that disciplinary measures are applied inconsistently due to bias, leading to hostile and unfair environments. Even though we see this in government statistics, there is no guidance to address this from the DfE – even in its updated *Suspension and Permanent Exclusions Guidance* published in September 2023 (DfE, 2023b).

In regard to all our policies, raising awareness, making inclusive transparent policy revisions and cultivating an atmosphere that values and accepts a range of identities within consistent guidelines are all necessary steps in ensuring equity and inclusion for all our students.

To address these issues, as educators we must become self aware of the part we play in prejudice, discrimination and oppression, engage in raising our own awareness of cultural issues and actively strive to be part of the change we wish to see. We should all be striving to create learning environments that respect and celebrate diversity, ensuring that all members of our school community feel that they belong, feel valued and are supported.

OUR DUTIES

It is important to understand our duties around teaching these concepts and why they are so important. I wrote this book because I strongly believe that teaching children about prejudice, discrimination and oppression from a young age is crucial for fostering a more inclusive society. It helps them develop empathy, critical thinking and social awareness. We can work towards a more equitable society by addressing these issues early. However, some believe that it is wrong to teach children these concepts. Pushback often arises because some believe children are too young to understand these complex topics or worry about indoctrination. However, age-appropriate education can lay the foundation for tolerance and understanding, reducing prejudice and discrimination in the long run. Children are observant. They notice differences in people, including race, from a young age. Research has shown that even if parents/carers and adults do not talk about race or other differences, children can still develop biases and prejudices. Therefore, having conversations with children about diversity, bias and prejudice is important. Awareness of difference does not automatically mean a child holds prejudice; I do not believe that. I think that pretending differences do not exist and not allowing children to explore these concepts in safe spaces with trained guides increases bias and discrimination.

Often, as adults, we have our discomfort around talking about differences, and we are so worried about being accused of discrimination that we shy away from difficult conversations around this. By having open discussions with children about diversity, bias and prejudice, we can help them develop a positive attitude towards differences in people. In an ever-increasing digital world, it is more and more difficult to shield our children from discrimination, so it is better to take an informed approach to tackling these subjects rather than only being reactive.

Knowing the laws around this will help you if you encounter any pushback around teaching these topics. Understanding legislation like the Human Rights Act 1998 and the Equality Act 2010 can help address resistance. The

Keeping Children Safe in Education (KCSIE) guidelines emphasise a school's responsibility to protect children from discrimination and abuse (DfE, 2023c). The Human Rights Act 1998 ensures that schools must not act in ways incompatible with the Convention on Human Rights, protecting essential rights.

KCSIE outlines what schools need to do to keep children safe. Every school has a responsibility to ensure that children are not exposed to prejudice, discrimination and oppression.

This right is covered under the following legislation:

- Human Rights Act 1998
- *Equality Act 2010: Advice for Schools* (DfE, 2018)
- *Public Sector Equality Duty* (MOJ, 2012)
- Public Sector Equality Duty (advice for schools) (ASCL, 2020).

Schools must have a joined-up approach to protecting children from becoming discriminated against based on their protected characteristics and being victims of abuse. KCSIE clearly states that the Public Sector Equality Duty places a general duty on schools and colleges to have, in the exercise of their functions, due regard to the need to eliminate unlawful discrimination, harassment and victimisation (and any other conduct prohibited under the Equality Act), to advance equality of opportunity and foster good relations between those who share a relevant protected characteristic and those who do not.

It also states that:

> Schools and colleges play a crucial role in preventative education. Preventative education is most effective in the context of a whole-school or college approach that prepares pupils and students for life in modern Britain and creates a culture of zero tolerance for sexism, misogyny/misandry, homophobia, biphobic and sexual violence/harassment.
>
> (DfE, 2023c, 131)

Each school must have a planned programme of evidence-based relationships and sex education (RSE) delivered in regularly timetabled lessons and reinforced throughout the whole curriculum. Such a programme should be fully inclusive and developed to the appropriate age and stage of development (especially when considering the needs of children with SEND and other vulnerabilities).

The programme must tackle, at an age-appropriate stage, issues such as:

- healthy and respectful relationships;
- boundaries and consent;
- stereotyping, prejudice and equality;
- body confidence and self-esteem;
- how to recognise an abusive relationship, including coercive and controlling behaviour;
- the concepts of and laws relating to: sexual consent, sexual exploitation, abuse, grooming, coercion, harassment, rape, domestic abuse, so-called 'honour'-based violence such as forced marriage and female genital mutilation (FGM) and how to access support; and
- what constitutes sexual harassment and sexual violence and why these are always unacceptable.

'Ultimately, all systems, processes and policies should operate with the *best interests* of the child at their heart' (DfE, 2023c, 95).

At the same time, the Human Rights Act 1998 (HRA) sets out the fundamental rights and freedoms that everyone in the UK is entitled to and contains the Articles and protocols of the European Convention on Human Rights (ECHR) (the Convention) that are deemed to apply in the UK.

Under the HRA, it is unlawful for schools and colleges to act in a way incompatible with the Convention. The specific Convention rights applying to schools and colleges are:

- *Article 3*: the right to freedom from inhuman and degrading treatment (an absolute right);
- *Article 8*: the right to respect for private and family life (a qualified right) includes a duty to protect individuals' physical and psychological integrity;
- *Article 14*: requires that all of the rights and freedoms set out in the Act must be protected and applied without discrimination; and
- *Protocol 1, Article 2*: protects the right to education.

Addressing prejudice, discrimination and oppression in children's education also aligns with British values, as outlined in the government's guidance for schools. These values include:

- *Democracy*: Teaching children to respect and value diversity is fundamental to democracy. It promotes the idea that everyone has a voice and should be treated fairly, regardless of background.

- *Rule of law*: Encouraging children to recognise and challenge discrimination and oppression contributes to a society based on the rule of law, where all individuals have equal rights and protection.
- *Individual liberty*: Promoting inclusivity and teaching children to tackle prejudice supports individual liberty by ensuring everyone is free to express themselves without fear of discrimination.
- *Mutual respect and tolerance*: Teaching children about different cultures, backgrounds and perspectives fosters mutual respect and tolerance. It helps create a society where people accept and value each other's differences.
- *Equality*: Addressing discrimination and oppression directly aligns with the principle of equality, emphasising that everyone should be treated fairly and without bias.

BULLYING

Learning about different types of bullying (including online) is now a statutory RSHE requirement. This consists of the impact of bullying, the responsibilities of bystanders to report bullying and how and where to get help.

This also crosses over with how to teach about abuse, harassment and discrimination within the PSHE education curriculum. PSHE Association guidance on 'Addressing bullying and discrimination in the curriculum' advises that schools should constantly tailor PSHE education to their pupils' needs (PSHE Association).

The DfE guidance states that:

> Schools are free to determine how to deliver the content in this guidance in the context of a broad and balanced curriculum. Effective teaching in these subjects will ensure that core knowledge is broken down into units of manageable size and communicated clearly to pupils, in a carefully sequenced way, within a planned programme or lessons.
>
> (DfE, 2021a, p. 8)

PAUSE FOR SELF-REFLECTION

- Why do you think it is important to teach children about prejudice, discrimination and oppression from a young age?

(Continued)

- Why do you think there is pushback when teaching children about these concepts?
- How can we ensure our teaching approaches are age-appropriate and inclusive?
- What strategies can we use to address resistance or pushback from parents/carers or colleagues when teaching these sensitive topics?
- How can you help create a culture of openness and zero tolerance for discrimination and prejudice, not just within your classroom but more widely across your school and wider school community?

At the end of this chapter, we have given you an example letter to share with parents and carers that you can adapt to your school context.

HOW DO WE TEACH IT?

Explaining complex concepts like prejudice, discrimination and oppression to children in simple terms is crucial because it ensures they can understand these ideas at their developmental level. Children can more easily empathise with others and appreciate the importance of fairness and kindness by using age-appropriate language and relatable examples. Simple explanations lay the groundwork for future, more in-depth discussions as children mature, fostering a lifelong understanding of these concepts. Additionally, clear and straightforward explanations prevent confusion or fear that might arise from complex language. Creating a safe space is important so all your children feel confident to ask questions and engage in ongoing conversations.

Simple stories, full of relatable examples, can help children understand these concepts and why being kind and fair to everyone is important.

First, start with why.

Explain to children that there are important lessons that help make the world a better place. When we understand these things, we can be kinder and fairer to everyone, no matter how different they are from us. Learning about prejudice helps us see that it's not okay to judge someone just because they're different, like having a different colour of skin or speaking a different language. Learning about discrimination teaches us that treating others unfairly because of those differences hurts people and isn't right. And when we learn about oppression, we see how some people can be very mean to others and not let them have the same chances in life, which isn't fair at all.

Explain to children that by learning about these things they will grow up to be caring and fair individuals who make the world a more equal and kinder place for everyone.

PREJUDICE

Prejudice is when someone doesn't like or is unkind to others just because they're different in some way, like having a favourite colour and not liking anyone who likes a different colour.

Some questions you might ask your students to help them consider this are:

- what does it mean to like or dislike someone just because they're different from us in some way?
- can you think of an example where someone was judged unfairly because of their differences?
- how can we learn to be more accepting of people who are different from us?

DISCRIMINATION

Discrimination is when people treat others unfairly because of those unkind feelings. It's like not letting someone join a game because they wear glasses, even though they're really good at playing.

Some questions you might use to help your students explore the concept of discrimination further:

- have you ever seen or experienced a situation where someone was treated unfairly because of who they are?
- how did it feel to witness or experience discrimination?
- what can we do to ensure everyone is treated fairly, regardless of their differences?

OPPRESSION

Oppression is when some people are mean to others and don't let them have the same chances or be themselves. It's like not letting someone choose their clothes or what they want to eat, which is unfair.

Some questions you might use to help your students explore the concept of oppression further:

- what does it mean when some people are mean to others and don't let them have the same chances or be themselves?
- have you ever felt like someone had power over you and treated you unfairly?
- how can we work together to make things fair when we witness oppression?

LESSON OR CLASSROOM ACTIVITIES

Rather than giving specific examples of how we can address these concepts, here are a range of activities for you to choose from. It's important to select the most appropriate ones for your school context, being mindful of recent events within the school community and beyond.

ACTIVITY

PREJUDICE, DISCRIMINATION AND OPPRESSION

- *Prejudice: diverse storytime*

  Read a storybook that features characters from different backgrounds, cultures, or abilities. Afterwards, discuss how it's important to be friends with and understand people who may seem different from us at first, but then show how we are all connected somehow.

- *Discrimination: barrier course*

  Set up an obstacle course where some children have obstacles while others have a clear path. Let the children experience the frustration of discrimination in this hands-on activity, and then discuss how it felt and why it's unfair.

- *Oppression: silent reflection*

  Have a moment of quiet reflection where children think about a time when they felt unfairly treated or left out. Encourage them to draw or write about it; discuss how it feels when someone has power over you and how we can work together to make things fair.

Some further activities to address these themes are:

- *Follow-up activities*

  Read a children's book that addresses themes of diversity, prejudice, or discrimination. Afterwards, engage in a group discussion about the story and its message. Encourage children to reflect on the story's lessons and how they can apply them in their own lives. Ask them to share instances where they've shown kindness and inclusivity.

- *Guided walk*

  Divide the class into pairs. One partner closes their eyes while the other guides them around the room. Then, switch roles. Discuss how it felt to rely on someone else and how this relates to empathy. Encourage children to think about situations where they can be more understanding and helpful towards others, especially those facing challenges. *Note*: If you have children in your class who are visually impaired it may not be appropriate to do this activity. If it is, be mindful not to rely on asking them to talk about their own experiences. It may be more appropriate to think of another activity.

- *Real-life examples*

  Share age-appropriate news stories or examples of positive actions to combat prejudice and discrimination. Discuss these stories with your children to reinforce the importance of fairness and inclusivity.

- *Role models*

  Introduce children to real-life role models who have made a difference by advocating for equality and social justice. Discuss their achievements and the positive impact they've had.

- *Conflict resolution*

  Teach children conflict resolution skills to help them navigate situations where prejudice or discrimination may arise. Encourage them to seek peaceful solutions and stand up for what's right.

- *Parent/carer and teacher collaboration*

  Collaborate with parents/carers and fellow educators to ensure a consistent message about these topics. Share resources and ideas for reinforcing these lessons at home and in the classroom.

- *Community engagement*

  Explore opportunities for your children to get involved in activities that promote inclusivity and equality in the community, such as participating in events or volunteering for causes they care about.

- *Continuous discussion*

  Keep the conversation going by periodically revisiting these topics. Encourage children to share their experiences and ongoing questions about prejudice, discrimination and oppression.

ACTIVITY

CHALLENGING ANTI-ATTITUDES

I use the word 'anti-attitudes' as a broader term with children and young people to describe negative discriminatory attitudes against particular people or groups. To me, it easily summarises a mindset that is resistant to reflection or change. We can only bring about change by acknowledging that we need to. Children and young people being able to speak up when they encounter anti-attitudes is an important part of teaching them to speak out and feel confident doing so.

Now that we've increased our own and our students' awareness of prejudice, discrimination and oppression, it's important to teach them how to report incidents. 'Stop, Speak, Support' is a tool devised by the charity Internet Matters to help children make smart choices online (see Further resources section of this chapter). You can adapt their original concept to encompass speaking out against all forms of prejudice, discrimination and oppression. These measures, when combined, demonstrate true allyship in action.

Stop. What is behind the behaviour? This means reflecting on and asking an adult to support a child/young person to investigate the reasons for these attitudes, including ignorance, fear and misinformation.

Speak (explain and educate). Education is a powerful tool against anti-attitudes. Providing accurate information and raising awareness of the negative effects of bias and discrimination can promote empathy and alter people's viewpoints.

Support. This is important, particularly for the individual or group who are being targeted. Showing support and solidarity towards people who are the target of discrimination shows them that they are not alone and that you are standing with them. Help to build and maintain support networks. This gives individuals the confidence to confront these views and find comfort in a supportive and understanding community.

Report. Reporting helps to hold perpetrators accountable, ensuring that this type of behaviour doesn't go unnoticed or without consequence. It also sends a message that these attitudes won't be tolerated in the immediate environment or in wider society, serving as a warning and deterrent for potential offenders. The whole point of reporting is to put a stop to the behaviour but to also help people reflect on their behaviour.

A SIMPLE GUIDE FOR CHILDREN

Table 5.1 Stop, speak, support

STOP	Pause the person with a simple response such as, 'It's not okay to say that' or 'You may not have meant to be unkind, but what you said is actually quite hurtful.'
SPEAK (EXPLAIN AND EDUCATE)	Be clear about why this is disrespectful and hurtful, and why they shouldn't be saying or doing it. You should also try to keep your explanation general, rather than using the person who it was aimed at as an example.
SUPPORT	If there was someone on the receiving end of the comment, show support for them. This does not mean making a point of how upset they are, as we have no way of knowing what others are really feeling, and shouldn't assume. However, you could check in with a simple, 'Are you okay?' afterwards.
REPORT	Report the incident to a teacher or trusted adult so that they are aware and can handle the situation properly. If you don't feel comfortable with others knowing that you reported the incident, you can always ask to remain anonymous.

CONCLUSION

Chapter 5 of this book delved into the critical topic of prejudice, discrimination and oppression. It emphasised the importance of introducing complex concepts like privilege, allyship and the bystander effect to children through broad and shared contexts. The chapter examined the various forms of prejudice and discrimination, underlining the significance of teaching these concepts from a young age to foster empathy, critical thinking and social awareness. It addresses concerns about pushback when teaching these topics and advocates for age-appropriate education to combat bias and discrimination effectively. The chapter also explores the legal aspects of teaching these concepts, highlighting key legislation such as the Human Rights Act 1998 and the Equality Act 2010, which emphasise the responsibility of schools to protect children from discrimination and abuse. It underscores the importance of a whole-school approach to preventative education and RSE programmes. The chapter aligns these efforts with British values and highlights the importance of democracy, the rule of law, individual liberty, mutual respect and tolerance, and equality.

We concluded with reflective questions for educators and practical strategies for addressing discrimination and promoting inclusivity. The chapter also explains complex concepts to children through age-appropriate language and activities, and how to challenge 'anti-attitudes' through understanding their root causes, education, support and reporting.

In the next chapter, we will examine the core concepts of equity and equality.

FURTHER READING AND RESOURCES

In general, you can use young children's understanding of differences to teach social justice through age-appropriate news stories and talking about examples they or you may have seen.

Some more specific resources are below.

Spiegler, J. (2016) Teaching young children about bias, diversity, and social justice. *Edutopia*. Available at: www.edutopia.org/blog/teaching-young-children-social-justice-jinnie-spiegler

Parker, K. (2022) How to tackle 'micro-aggressions' in your school. *Tes Magazine*. Available at: www.tes.com/magazine/teaching-learning/general/how-tackle-micro-aggressions-your-school

Anna Freud (n.d.) Anti-racism and mental health resources: Micro-aggressions. Available at: https://mentallyhealthyschools.org.uk/resources/anti-racism-and-mental-health-resources-microaggressions/

Internet Matters (n.d.) Stop, Speak, Support explained. Available at: www.internetmatters.org/issues/cyberbullying/stop-speak-support/stop-speak-support-parent-advice/

DfE (2017) *Preventing and Tackling Bullying: Advice for Headteachers, Staff and Governing Bodies.* Available at: https://assets.publishing.service.gov.uk/government/uploads/system/uploads/attachment_data/file/1069688/Preventing_and_tackling_bullying_advice.pdf

Perkins, H.W., Craig, D.W. and Perkins, J.M. (2011) Using social norms to reduce bullying: A research intervention among adolescents in five middle schools. *Group Processes and Intergroup Relations*, 14(5), 703–22. https://doi.org/10.1177/1368430210398004

Dutta, M.J. (2019) How to challenge racism by listening to those who experience it. *The Conversation.* Available at: https://theconversation.com/how-to-challenge-racism-by-listening-to-those-who-experience-it-113909

LETTER TO PARENTS/CARERS

Note: This should come from the head of school/headteacher and chair of governors, if appropriate, not the class teacher. It is meant as an example. Therefore, it must be edited to include your school values and modified to fit your school context.

Dear parents/carers,

Re: Teaching concepts around tackling prejudice, discrimination and oppression

I hope this letter finds you well. I am writing to explain the approach we are taking at [school name] in teaching your children topics related to tackling prejudice, discrimination and oppression.

At [school name], we are committed to providing a well-rounded and inclusive education for all our students. We believe that addressing these important social issues is an educational responsibility and a moral imperative. Here's why we are taking this approach.

1. *Promoting inclusivity*: Teaching our students about prejudice, discrimination and oppression from a young age helps foster a more inclusive and accepting school community. It equips them with the knowledge and skills to appreciate diversity and treat everyone respectfully.

2. *Developing critical thinking*: These topics encourage critical thinking and empathy. By exploring real-world examples and discussing the consequences of discrimination and prejudice, we aim to nurture well-rounded individuals who can think critically about the world around them.
3. *Compliance with legislation*: We must comply with relevant legislation, including the Human Rights Act 1998 and the Equality Act 2010, which require schools to promote equality and prevent discrimination. Teaching these topics aligns with our legal obligations.
4. *Preventing bias and stereotypes*: Research shows that children can develop biases and stereotypes even without explicit discussions. By addressing these issues openly, we aim to prevent the formation of harmful biases and stereotypes among our students.
5. *Digital-age challenges*: Children are exposed to various forms of discrimination and bias through media and the internet in today's digital world. Our approach ensures students are prepared to navigate these challenges and understand the importance of respectful and responsible online behaviour.

We believe that by teaching these topics in a sensitive and age-appropriate manner, we can contribute to developing compassionate and informed individuals who will positively contribute to society.

We will be using the following resources; you are welcome to come in to view these or find a link to further information here [insert link].

(You could also mention this book!)

We understand some parents/carers may have concerns or questions about this approach. We are committed to open communication and welcome any discussions or feedback you may have. Don't hesitate to contact us at [contact information] to discuss this further.

Thank you for your continued support in ensuring that [school name] remains a safe and inclusive learning environment for all our students.

Yours sincerely,
[headteacher's name]
Headteacher

6

WHAT IS ADVOCACY AND HOW DO WE USE IT BOTH TO PROMOTE EQUITY AND REMOVE INEQUALITY?

KEY CONCEPTS

The key concepts covered in this chapter are:

- what is advocacy and how can we use it to show we are true allies?
- what is the difference between equality and equity, and why is this distinction so important?
- what is intersectionality and how does this link to allyship?
- how can we foster a sense of belonging in our schools and workplaces?

INTRODUCTION

In this chapter, we will look at the concepts of advocacy, equity and equality. When thinking about how we use advocacy to promote equity and remove inequality, we need to make distinctions between these two actions.

Advocacy and *allyship* are concepts rooted in the pursuit of justice and fairness, playing pivotal roles in the ongoing conversation surrounding equality and equity. Despite the fact that these concepts are often used interchangeably, they stand for different ideals.

On the one hand, equality's goal is to make sure that all people receive the same treatment and have access to the same opportunities and resources.

It's about ensuring everyone is treated identically even if, as individuals, they have different needs.

On the other hand, equity recognises that not everyone begins from the same starting point and disadvantages can be caused by a person's immediate environment, by systemic and historical factors or all of these. Equity recognises that these disadvantages must be addressed to ensure that everyone has an equal chance at success. Different levels of support or resources may be required depending on each person's individual needs. Providing different levels of support is the only way to ensure that everyone is given the necessary support to succeed.

Advocacy is simple, but it is a term that can get overcomplicated. What are you passionate about and prepared to speak up about? Have you ever written a letter of complaint, signed a petition, publicly supported a cause on social media or made a speech about something important to you? That's advocacy in its simplest form. We show solidarity with others when we *stand up*, *speak up* and *speak out* for them; that's advocacy.

For me, my advocacy is my passion to speak out for the rights of children and ensuring that I represent children who cannot speak up for themselves – especially children from marginalised groups that face higher levels of discrimination due to their race and disabilities. I am passionate about this due to my own experiences, the experiences of my children and those in my care as an educator. Many families of disabled children don't know the system, so they don't know whether their child is getting the support they should at school. I get contacted by parents/carers asking me to check their rights for them as they know I have the experience to understand what good support should look like. When my children were younger, I used to ask other people's advice and they used to help me; that's why I feel it's important to help others. That's advocacy. In the book *Why We Act* by Catherine A. Sanderson (2022), the author talks about how to 'turn bystanders into moral rebels' and how we can learn how to act. The second part of the book specifically looks at 'bullies and bystanders' and how we can understand/misunderstand bullying.

Bullying is a huge issue in our schools, and it can sometimes feel like it might take a lot to change a school culture around this. Sanderson argues that bullying behaviour can be altered through:

1. challenging social norms and influence through the power of social connections;
2. building stronger connections between students and teachers.

In the section on fostering ethical behaviour at work, Sanderson talks about why people ignore bad behaviour, specifically what she calls the 'professional benefits of staying silent'.

What are people's motives for overlooking bad behaviour? Some people know what is happening and choose to look the other way. Sanderson believes that: 'Most of us would make the same choice if we found ourselves in their shoes because the professional consequences of calling someone out for bad behaviour can be substantial, especially if that person is in a powerful position' (2022, p. 138).

This was my experience in a former workplace. People chose to stay silent about my treatment rather than show allyship towards me, even though they knew the behaviour was wrong. They felt too intimidated to speak out for fear of reprisals. They chose to protect themselves. A handful of people did tell me that they knew I was right, they had witnessed or experienced what I had spoken up about themselves. What did they all have in common? They had either left or were in the process of leaving the organisation so did not feel as much fear.

I read an article once that should have been titled, 'Beware of workplaces that call themselves a family'. It was, in fact, called 'Why your business isn't a "family"' (Abbas, 2023). The irony was that nepotism was rife in my former organisation, which made for a very toxic experience. The article stated:

> Families rely on loyalty. Companies that consider themselves families are likelier to expect unquestioned loyalty from employees. Loyalty creates camaraderie, but, depending on who's in charge, it can also be toxic and blinding in family-like organizations. Here are some examples:
>
> - Hazing by fraternities and sororities.
> - Criminal acts by terrorist groups.
> - Murders by the mafia.
> - Deaths at the hands of crazed cult leaders.

Companies that consider themselves families may unwittingly foster an 'us vs them' mentality – you're either in the family or you're not. And this can get ugly in the workplace through:

- **Discrimination and bias**: People who don't look or act like the family (your company, team or division, etc.) won't be trusted or hired.

- **Groupthink**: Employees will only say what they think the 'family' wants to hear, instead of challenging the status quo. This thinking can stifle new ideas and innovation.
- **Bad judgment**: Organizations that function like families might be more willing to forgive and forget offences that can seriously compromise the entire business (e.g., financial fraud, harassment and bad management).

(Abbas, 2023)

Workplaces like this strongly emphasise loyalty, which makes the cost of standing up or betraying that loyalty even higher. No one wants to be ostracised by their families. Indeed, ostracisation is a common method used in making someone stay silent. All you have to do is make them feel like an outsider. 'Toxic environments often grow gradually, as unethical behaviour starts with something small, but then continues and expands' (Abbas, 2023). You are more likely to support someone from the same dominant group as you, even if you know that person is deeply flawed, than to switch your loyalties to an outsider.

FOSTERING A SENSE OF COLLECTEDNESS/BELONGING

Students who report being close to their families are more likely to say they would intervene to stop bullying. This was highlighted in a 2019 study published by *the Journal of Youth and Adolescence* (Mulvey et al., 2019). Our families are meant to be our first advocates. Good parents and carers know when to advocate for their children. This is something that families of children from marginalised groups understand all too well as they are more likely to have to advocate on their children's behalf.

Advocates and allies that are effective go above and beyond just providing assistance; they actively take the time to understand the obstacles that marginalised people or groups encounter. Allies pay attention, stay informed and make use of their position to raise the voices of people they support. Being an ally is more than simply showing up; it's about opposing prejudice and actively fighting for justice, equity, diversity and inclusion (JEDI).

The opposite to inclusion is exclusion. We know that bias can lead to actions that perpetuate discrimination rather than addressing harmful behaviours that cause the discrimination in the first instance. For example, when promoting a cause, a biased advocate may unintentionally reinforce stereotypes or prejudiced viewpoints. Furthermore, a prejudiced ally may not have a true understanding of the struggles and difficulties of the marginalised group they are standing up for. It could be argued that it is impossible for allies to truly understand without lived experience. That is why self-awareness is so important for educators. Reflecting on ourselves and our actions demonstrates that we are committed to continually challenging and re-educating ourselves so that we don't inadvertently share what could be harmful biases with our students.

INTERSECTIONALITY

> If you see inequality as their problem or unfortunate other problem, that is a problem.
>
> Kimberlé Crenshaw, Civil rights advocate, intersectional feminist, and lawyer.

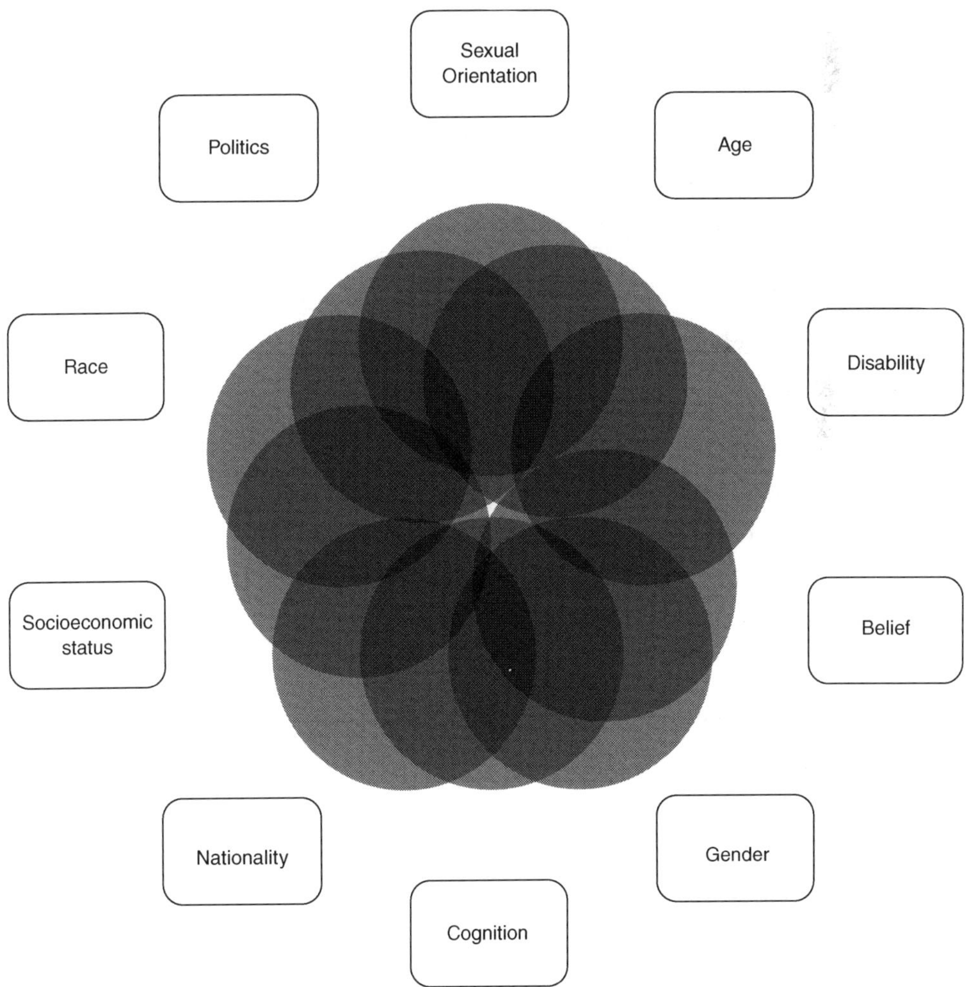

Figure 6.1 Venn diagram of intersectionality

'Intersectionality' is a term coined by Kimberlé Crenshaw. Crenshaw introduced the concept of intersectionality in her essay titled 'Mapping the margins: Intersectionality, identity politics, and violence against women of color' (Crenshaw, 1991). It highlights that rather than being separate, our social identities are interconnected as we all belong to multiple categories, such as gender, class, sexuality and race. Crenshaw uses the concept to talk about her identity as a Black gay female and how these identities intersect. Crenshaw talks about individual experiences around privilege and discrimination and how our identity impacts our lived experiences.

The term has now been adapted to discuss all intersectionality, not just from the starting point of race. Some argue that the word existed before Crenshaw adapted it and that it is important to use it for all intersectionality, much like the rhetoric of 'all lives matter' rather than 'Black lives matter'. Some criticism revolves around the fact that it emphasises specific aspects of identity; it should be used broadly to highlight all social injustices and inequalities. The former makes people feel they are being pitted against each other rather than supporting each other.

Similarly, some of the criticism around this book is that it does not just focus on racism. My own experiences made me want to focus this book on supporting victims of all forms of discrimination. Discrimination on the grounds of race and disability is my personal experience but I know of many other people who have had to deal with being marginalised and discriminated against based on who they love, how they choose to live their lives in regard to their sexuality, or gender.

It may be that a part of their identity doesn't cause them to be discriminated against in some parts of the UK, and others do. If they do encounter discrimination, they may be protected by law in the UK but not in other parts of the world where law does not protect them. Therefore, understanding the term 'intersectionality' and the debate for and against its use helps us know and raise awareness about the diversity of human experiences. This allows us to develop empathy towards other social groups that do not share our identities or lived experiences.

PAUSE FOR SELF-REFLECTION

- How have you been an advocate and shown up for other people?
- When have you chosen not to be an advocate, and stayed silent instead?
- Has this book helped you to reflect?
- How do you feel now?

- What will you do to change your behaviour going forward?
- Why is it important for children and young people to be advocates?

HOW DO WE TEACH CHILDREN TO BE EFFECTIVE ADVOCATES?

CHILDREN'S RIGHTS

We will now talk about how to teach children about their rights and those of other people, especially those who cannot stand up for themselves.

Children's rights are the basic human rights that all children are entitled to regardless of their race, gender, nationality, or any other status. These rights were agreed upon at the United Nations Convention on the Rights of the Child (UNCRC) (1989). They are meant to ensure that children's rights are protected globally.

These rights include:

- the right to life;
- the right to education;
- the right to be free from violence and abuse;
- the right to have a say in decisions that affect you.

But when we look at what's happening in the world around us, it seems that some children are given more rights than others. This is often the case in war and conflict, where authorities will support one country to defend themselves over another. It is confusing for children, and they may well ask why the children in one area of the world seem to matter to the world more than the children in another. It's hard to teach about unfairness like this. Why do a child's rights vary depending on geopolitical factors?

UNICEF does try to explain this in its resources around discussing war and conflict in class, and how to talk to children about war and conflict (UNICEF, 2023).

HOW DO WE TEACH CHILDREN TO USE ADVOCACY TO PROTECT THEIR RIGHTS, PROMOTE EQUITY AND REMOVE INEQUALITY?

Teaching children about advocacy is a powerful way to instil a sense of responsibility towards protecting their rights and others. Everyone should have a deeply embedded sense of purpose to show them why they matter. Sometimes we just don't know it yet.

It involves:

- listening;
- advocating for yourself;
- protecting your rights;
- offering practical support;
- challenging unfair decisions;
- speaking up against discrimination;
- supporting others to make the right decisions.

It is important to make people feel empowered to become advocates. It's not easy work and takes a lot of courage over time. Most people don't become advocates until something happens to make them think, then they realise how important it is. We can teach children to be advocates by showing them examples of advocate role models that they can look up to.

We can do this by:

- encouraging their self-expression;
- leading by example;
- getting them involved in community engagement and activism;
- building their critical thinking;
- giving them opportunities to collaborate and support one another.

DR SEUSS

> Unless someone like you cares a whole awful lot,
>
> Nothing is going to get better. It's not.
>
> Dr Seuss, *The Lorax*, 1971

The children's author Dr Seuss often used his books to convey important messages about advocacy, equality and social issues. In *Horton Hears a Who!* (1954) Dr Seuss emphasises the importance of advocating for the rights and voices of even the smallest and most marginalised members of society. The famous line, 'A person's a person, no matter how small' underscores the value of every individual and the need to stand up for those who may not have a strong voice (Dr Seuss, 1954, p. 7).

But whose role is it anyway?

Dr Seuss's work often encourages readers, including children, to be advocates for positive change, to stand up against injustice and to protect the world and its inhabitants. We can use his books to show children that every one of us has a role to play, individually or collectively, in creating a better world for everyone.

By being better allies, all children and young people can improve the world we live in. Children may think they are too young, but helping them recognise the significance of their role is essential.

LESSON OR CLASSROOM ACTIVITIES

The following activity provides opportunities for children to learn about their own agency. A number of scenarios are suggested – or you can adapt the activity and use your own scenario.

ACTIVITY

THE FOUR CORNERS SCENARIO: WILL YOU CHOOSE TO BE AN ALLY OR A BYSTANDER?

OBJECTIVE

The *four corners* activity is a well-known interactive exercise often used in advocacy training to engage participants in discussing various perspectives or positions on an issue.

EQUIPMENT

- A room or space with four identifiable corners
- Four pieces of A4/A3 paper or card with the corner labels written on them as demonstrated in Figure 6.2
- Scenarios
- Cleared space (big enough for the class to be comfortable to move around in)

Figure 6.2 Four corners activity

INSTRUCTIONS

Participants are given four choices, and each corner represents one of these choices.

1. Ignore the situation or walk away.
2. Step in myself.
3. Talk to the person by themselves.
4. Get help from an adult or someone older than you.

For each scenario, say: 'You decide, what should you do? Sometimes, you might do something. Sometimes, you might not.'

It often depends on:

- the situation;
- how well you know someone;
- if they are older or younger;
- if it's dangerous to intervene.

POSSIBLE SCENARIOS

Below is a selection of possible scenarios based on protected characteristics. Choose a scenario to get the class started with this activity. You can also add ones that you have made up or that the pupils give you. Some children like to share real-life scenarios. It is important again to emphasise that the classroom is a safe space for them to do so, but this needs to be handled sensitively, and they may need further support after this.

AGE/SIZE

- A classmate or friend constantly makes fun of another student because they are small for their age.
- An older student makes fun of a younger student because they are small for their age.
- At break time, you hear two other students calling someone a horrible name.
- Your friend teases another student because their trousers are too small.

GENDER EXPRESSION/GENDER IDENTITY

- When you are with a group of friends, one of them makes fun of a younger student because of the way they dress.
- A friend of yours keeps saying to other boys, 'Hey, stop acting like a girl.'
- A boy in your school you don't know very well keeps saying to other boys, 'Hey, stop acting like a girl.'
- A friend in your class teases a younger boy for having a teddy bear or a doll.
- A student in your class teases a boy for wearing a pink t-shirt and nail polish.
- A girl in your class teases another girl for always dressing 'like a boy'.
- A friend of yours keeps asking a new student if they are a boy or a girl.

RACE/ETHNICITY/CULTURAL IDENTITY

- A new kid at school calls your friend a bad name because of their skin colour.
- A friend of yours calls a new kid at school a bad name because of their skin colour.
- A kid you don't know calls another kid you don't remember a bad name because of their skin colour.
- You hear another classmate tease a new student about what they are wearing. The student is wearing traditional clothing from their home country.
- You see two students making fun of another child's school lunch because it has food different from what their family eats.

DISABILITY

- Your friend teases another student for not being in the same math group.
- You see two kids teasing another student because they are reading 'baby books'.
- You notice that a student in a wheelchair is not included in basketball or four-square during break time.
- You notice that no one picks a certain student for their team during physical education because they have trouble moving quickly.

WHO YOU LOVE/FAMILIES

- A new kid at school calls your friend 'gay'.
- A group of students your age keeps saying 'that's gay' to mean they don't like something.
- A group of students your age keeps saying 'that's gay' to mean they don't like something, and you know that your friend's dads are gay.
- Your classmate has two mums, and you hear a child ask them which one is their real mum.
- You hear a classmate ask another student, 'Why do you have such a big family?'
- You hear a classmate ask another student, 'Why don't the people in your family match?'

SOCIOECONOMIC LEVEL

- You see two kids making fun of another child because they don't eat school lunches.
- You hear a child acting shocked that another student's family doesn't own a computer.
- A classmate comments negatively about the old car someone's parent/carer drives.

MULTILINGUALISM/HOME LANGUAGE

- You see two kids making fun of/copying another student's accent/way of talking.
- Your friend angrily tells another student they should return to where they came from.

RELIGION

- Someone in your class says something mean to another student in your school because of their religion.
- A kid you don't know asks another student why they don't celebrate a certain holiday.
- You see two kids making fun of another student for the clothing that their family wears that is part of their religious expression (for example, hijab, head scarf).

REFLECTION

The four corners activity can be a fantastic way to introduce children and young people to different perspectives in a fun and interactive manner.

It's not just about moving around a room; it's a journey of exploration, learning and empowerment, laying the foundation for a future generation that values and embraces diverse perspectives.

By physically moving to different corners, children get to express their viewpoints and absorb the diversity of opinions held by their peers. This active participation makes complex concepts more tangible and relatable, encouraging them to think critically about various scenarios.

Witnessing the animated discussions and seeing children open up about their reasoning is inspiring. It highlights the value of providing a safe space for expression, where each opinion is respected and considered. Repeating the activity using different scenarios can allow your students to express themselves confidently, nurturing their communication skills and boosting their self-esteem. It works particularly well as a reflection exercise after an incident has occurred.

The beauty of this activity is its ability to introduce complex topics in a simplified, engaging manner, nurturing an understanding of diverse perspectives and the importance of respectful dialogue. It can be a starting point for deeper conversations and encourages children to approach differences openly, fostering empathy and appreciation for different opinions.

CONCLUSION

By integrating discussions on equality and equity into the exploration of advocacy and allyship, this chapter has underlined the importance of equal and fair treatment. It's not merely about offering the same opportunities to everyone, but also about addressing systemic barriers that hinder certain groups from accessing them. In the educational context, this understanding becomes pivotal.

Bullying is an issue that can significantly impact both the educational and workplace environment. It is, therefore, an essential aspect to consider when discussing advocacy, allyship, equality and equity. Integrating discussions on these principles directly addresses the root causes of bullying and its detrimental effects on individuals and the school community.

We emphasise the importance of addressing power imbalances and systemic issues often contributing to bullying scenarios. It's not just about punishing the act but understanding the dynamics that lead to such behaviour. Advocacy and allyship play critical roles in not just supporting victims but in fostering a culture that prevents and addresses bullying at its core.

Education should be about creating an environment that doesn't just treat everyone the same but acknowledges and responds to the diverse needs of all our students. By intertwining the concepts of advocacy, allyship, equality and equity within the educational framework, this chapter has strived to lay the groundwork for a generation that not only comprehends these concepts but actively contributes towards a more just and equitable society – within the classroom and also within local communities and beyond.

FURTHER READING AND RESOURCES

The Rights of the Child: Law and Practice by Michael Freeman
Children's Rights: A Very Short Introduction by Jonathan Todres and Cindy Blackstock
Children's Rights: Today's Global Challenge edited by Philip Alston
The United Nations Convention on the Rights of the Child: A Commentary edited by John Tobin

FOR CHILDREN

We Are All Born Free: The Universal Declaration of Human Rights in Pictures by Amnesty International
Children Just Like Me: A Unique Celebration of Children Around the World by Anabel Kindersley and Barnabas Kindersley
Let's Talk About Race by Julius Lester (covers issues related to equality and human rights)
If the World Were a Village: A Book about the World's People by David J. Smith (touches on global diversity and human rights)
We Dream of a World: Children's Ideas for a Better World by the Global Fund for Children

7

TEACHING ALLYSHIP THROUGH KINDNESS AND COMPASSION

KEY CONCEPTS

The key concepts covered in this chapter are:

- what it takes to be a superhero;
- how we can use the concept of superheroes to explore the concepts of allyship through kindness and compassion;
- using familiar and everyday examples to demonstrate how to be a superhero.

INTRODUCTION

This chapter looks at how we can use the ideas of superheroes to talk about kindness, compassion and how this leads to allyship. Every superhero has two sides. The quiet, unassuming side; then the strong, confident and powerful side when they get changed. Superheroes are still the same person but putting on a costume helps them to be more confident.

Being an ally is a bit like being a superhero. It means that even if we're not feeling particularly strong or brave, we can still stand up for others when they need us. Being an ally starts with kindness, standing up for people, whether they are our friends or not.

When I was younger, I loved Wonder Woman (I still do). Wonder Woman (Diana Prince) is a warrior with a strong sense of justice and compassion. She teaches important lessons about empathy, understanding and fighting for what's right.

Here are some other examples:

Spider-Man (Peter Parker) is known for his friendly and kind nature. He helps people in his community and stands up for what's right, all while dealing with the challenges of being a regular teenager.

Ms Marvel (Kamala Khan) is a relatable superhero for young readers. She's a teenager who cares about her family, friends and her community. She uses her shape-shifting powers to help others and promote unity.

Ant-Man (Scott Lang) is a single father who wants to be a good role model for his daughter. He uses his shrinking and growing abilities to help others and protect his loved ones.

Supergirl (Kara Zor-El) is a symbol of hope and compassion. She's a strong and caring hero who strives to make the world a better place, and she often works to inspire others.

Shazam (Billy Batson) When young Billy Batson says the word 'Shazam', he transforms into an adult superhero. Despite his powers, he retains his childlike heart and enthusiasm, always aiming to do good.

Black Panther (T'Challa) is the king of Wakanda. He is wise, compassionate and deeply cares for his people. T'Challa is not only a powerful superhero but also a thoughtful leader who wants to create a better world. He's a great example of using one's strengths to protect and uplift others.

PAUSE FOR SELF-REFLECTION

- We all have heroes, but what makes them *super*heroes?
- Do you have a favourite superhero? Have a think so that you can discuss them with your class.
- Who are the heroes in your life? What did they do to support you? How did they show allyship towards you?

WHY SUPERHEROES?

EMPATHY

Superheroes demonstrate a strong sense of empathy and understanding towards others. They show care and consideration for the wellbeing of their friends, allies and even strangers.

KINDNESS

They regularly do acts of kindness, whether it's helping a friend in need, supporting someone who's struggling, or promoting inclusivity and understanding.

COURAGE

Superheroes are known for their courage and willingness to stand up for what's right, even in the face of challenges. Their bravery inspires us to overcome our own fears and take action when needed.

TEAMWORK

They work together with others and support one another. The power of collaboration and collective efforts can lead to positive change.

INCLUSIVITY

They value inclusivity and embrace diversity. They're allies to individuals from various backgrounds and abilities, highlighting the importance of treating everyone with respect and fairness.

SELFLESSNESS

They prioritise the wellbeing of others over their own needs or desires. Their selfless actions encourage children to consider how their actions can positively impact those around them.

GROWTH AND LEARNING

When superheroes acquire their powers, they have to learn to adapt and develop. They learn from their experiences and mistakes.

LEADING BY EXAMPLE

We can look up to them as examples of how everyone can make a positive impact on their communities. How can we show and share these qualities with others? Qualities like listening, speaking up, trying new things, making an effort to include everyone, sharing, helping, showing and treating others with respect, learning from mistakes.

HOW DO WE USE SUPERHEROES TO TEACH CHILDREN ALLYSHIP?

Ask your students who their favourite superheroes are and why.

What do they like about their character? How do they show kindness and allyship?

Discuss what qualities they have in common that make them good allies.

Below, you will read the story of Baanab. It is about a child who goes on a journey of self-discovery to find what kindness means but discovers that the power of kindness is right there, within them all along. Baanab grows from being a shy and overlooked individual to an everyday hero who harnesses the innate power of kindness to create a brighter world for themselves and those around them.

The story of Baanab came about when I was trying to explain to my own children why kindness is so important. I wanted Baanab to be a character that anyone could relate to. To me, being an ally is fundamentally about being kind and showing compassion towards others. Superheroes selflessly help other people, people they don't even know, because they feel morally driven to do so. It is their purpose, their reason for being. As we've learnt in other chapters, storytelling is a powerful way to explain abstract concepts and deepen understanding. Hopefully, through this story, your students will gain a better understanding of why allyship is so important and how everyday actions that might seem little actually have huge importance.

MEET BAANAB!

Baanab doesn't like school. There was always someone who wanted to start trouble for literally no reason at all!

They'd be like, 'Hey, why are you looking at me like that?' when Baanab wasn't looking at them at all! Or they'd yell, 'Move, you're in my way!' when Baanab was nowhere near them. Sometimes, Baanab wished they could just disappear. Baanab wanted to be invisible, just like superheroes are. Baanab always remembered what Nana said, 'Just be kind, Baanab, they don't know how special you are. One day they'll see.'

'One day,' Baanab would mutter under their breath. 'One day.'

Baanab did have some friends at school, but they didn't always want to do the same things at break time. This meant that sometimes Baanab would end up all alone at lunch; they couldn't even find friends at the special 'friendship table'!

Every day after school, their family would ask, 'How was your day?' and every day, Baanab would give the same response, 'Fine!' before going to their room. Baanab couldn't wait for school to end, they were counting down the days. But they didn't want to be an adult either, having to pay their own bills and work! No way!

One day, while Baanab was daydreaming in class, the teacher said they had something serious to say. It was usually not that serious, it was usually something like someone had forgotten to tuck in their chairs, so they were all going to miss break time or someone had taken the class ruler without asking, so no pudding for a week. Or, worse still, someone had forgotten to put the lid back on the glue stick, so it had dried up!

But this time, Baanab sensed it was different. Baanab's teacher began to talk.

'We've noticed that sometimes people aren't being as kind as they could be to each other. For example, there are some of you that are not letting other people join in at break times. They tell their friends not to talk to other people that they're not usually friends with and are saying horrible things online after school.

That's not how we expect people to be in our school.'

'So, tomorrow, we're going to be doing a kindness hunt. We're going to look out for people throughout the day that are doing kind things to help other people.

For every kind thing someone does, they will earn one pebble for our pebble jar. The person who has contributed the most pebbles will get to choose a special activity for the class to do instead of a normal lesson.'

'Remember, you won't know who has the most pebbles throughout the day. We expect you to think about what kindness means and make more of an effort to show it to each other.'

'What does kindness mean?' thought Baanab.

As usual, their teacher had thought everyone understood, but didn't ask. 'I'm not going to bother,' Baanab thought. 'What's the point? I never get chosen for anything anyway.'

'We've sent a letter home to all your families to ask them to share with us what kind things you do at home too,' Baanab's teacher continued.

The next day, Baanab woke up earlier than everyone else but not as early as their little brother, Ada. He was always up early, trying to sneak on someone's phone to play games, or trying to eat biscuits for breakfast.

As usual, Baanab helped their little brother – helped him get washed, changed and sat down with him for breakfast.

'Shush,' Baanab said to him, 'Nana's having a lie in.'

Baanab then made a cup of tea for Nana, a cup of Earl Grey with milk and honey just as she liked it and took it upstairs. She was starting to wake up when Banaab gently said. 'Don't worry, we're ready for school. We've had breakfast, and I've washed up. We've run out of bread, though, so I'll get some on my way home.'

'My little hero,' Nana said, half asleep.

Baanab walked their brother to school. On the way, they noticed a mother struggling with a pram. She said, 'Excuse me, can you let me through?' but no one listened so Baanab repeated it for her, and they were able to get past.

Baanab took their brother to his class and helped him choose a new reading book to take home. Baanab hadn't really enjoyed reading it but knew it would help Ada to get better at reading.

Baanab went round to their own class. Someone had dropped their coat on the floor, so Baanab picked it up and put it across the pegs.

When they got to class, Baanab helped give the pencils out for morning spellings and went to sit down.

The whole day was like that. Baanab doing little things to help other people. But Baanab was just being Baanab. Just an ordinary day.

At the end of the day, Baanab's teacher called the class together and told them they were going to have a talk about the kindness challenge. Baanab had forgotten about that.

Baanab's teacher praised the class for being kind.

'Class, I want to say well done to everybody for trying really hard to be kind today. There were so many times that we noticed people doing things for other people and that's what kindness is.'

But Baanab thought, 'This is just me, no big deal.'

'Class, kindness is a power that we all possess. It's a simple act that can fill someone's day with sunshine by making their day brighter – a smile, a helping hand, or a thoughtful gesture. It's about looking out for each other, understanding that even small actions can have a big impact.

'Kindness turns ordinary moments into extraordinary ones. It's something that we all can share with each other.'

'Class, imagine allyship as a force, superpowered by kindness. Just like superheroes team up to make the world a better place, kindness works hand in hand with allyship. It's about standing up for one another and offering support when it's needed most. Kindness becomes a shield against negativity, and allyship gives us the strength to stand together, to break down barriers. A kind word, a show of solidarity, these are the qualities that make us all superheroes. Allyship boosts kindness into a super force for good. If we use it together, we can reshape and unite our world.' Baanab, chuckled. Their teacher was always so extra.

'It's been so lovely catching you all being so good, but the nicest thing has been the feedback that we've had from families, from parents and carers at home, who told us what a lovely idea it is for us to have a kindness day. I wanted to read you one little note.'

It says 'I just wanted to say thank you for having a kindness day. I know that it will be an opportunity for my sweet grandchild to show everybody how kind they are.'

'I had a bad accident a while back and I can't do things as easily as I used to. They do so much for me at home, helping me with the little one and doing things around the house. They don't go out much because I need help. They are the kindest child I know.'

The other kids looked at each other. Some grinned, and others rolled their eyes. Baanab's teacher continued reading the note.

'You're very lucky to have them in your school and I hope other people see that too.'

The note was signed:

From

A. Kind

The class gasped and started whispering to each other. A. Kind? As in 'One of A Kind', the local hero?

Wasn't that the famous wrestler? The one that was forced to retire early after refusing to carry on a fight after their opponent had been injured? They were a local hero! Everyone still talked about her! The opponent had been badly injured after someone threw a chair into the ring. Standing up for someone who couldn't stand up for themselves was a big deal in their community. One of A Kind had picked their injured opponent up and carried them out of the arena to get some help. It had been all over the news everywhere! Everyone in their town knew the story of the local hero A. Kind.

Baanab had heard the story so many times but didn't think everyone else knew it. They sat up a bit straighter.

Baanab's teacher continued; the class were excited now!

'Other people have told me that they've seen Baanab do some lovely things too, always helping other people. So, thank you Baanab; our first pebble in our jar is because of you.'

The class started whispering excitedly to each other. One of A Kind was Baanab's nan!

One of their classmates put their hand up. 'Can I add a pebble for Baanab?'

'This is for when you got the pencils out for everyone this morning.'

Baanab smiled.

Another pupil put their hand up. 'This is for getting me a drink when I started coughing in class this morning.'

Another pupil put their hand up, then another and another. All sharing stories of how Baanab had helped them.

Baanab felt something so warm inside! They felt themselves glowing with pride. Kindness day had been the best day ever.

Baanab ran all the way home. They had almost forgotten to pick Ada up from his class too. When they got home, Baanab gave Nana the biggest squeeze ever. 'Thank you, Nana.'

'No, thank you, Baanab; you make me so proud every day. Sometimes other people may not see how special you are. But I do and I wanted everyone to know.'

Baanab described the warm feeling and how it had lit up inside them.

'I loved that feeling!' Baanab said. 'It's the best in the world.'

'I told you so,' Nana said. 'But I wanted you to feel it for yourself. Not only does it make you feel good, but it comes from making others feel good too. There's nothing better than that.'

From that day on, Baanab knew that being kind was a superpower and vowed to do everything to help that feeling grow. And guess what? You can be a kindness superhero too, just like Baanab!

LESSON OR CLASSROOM ACTIVITIES

The first of the following classroom activities focuses on acts of kindness. Children are given the opportunity to create their own story of kindness. The second activity is a 'hunt for kindness' that encourages children to find kindness around them.

ACTIVITY

BAANAB

OBJECTIVE

In this activity, your students will use the story of Baanab to inspire their own stories. They will create their own story around acts of kindness, the first step towards being an allyship superhero.

INSTRUCTIONS

1. Explain the task.
2. Discussion.
3. Read the story to the class.
4. Give them time to answer the comprehension questions.
5. Get them started in creating their own stories: 'What happens next in the adventures of Baanab? How does Baanab use their superpowers to help others, just like an ally?'
6. Sharing and discussion.
7. Reflection.

COMPREHENSION QUESTIONS

Who:

1. Who is the main character of the story and what is their name?
2. Who gives Baanab advice about kindness and what is the advice?
3. Who is A. Kind and why is their note significant to the class?

What:

1. What does Baanab's teacher announce to the class that they will be doing? Why is this activity important?
2. What are some examples of kind acts that Baanab does throughout the day?

3. What does Nana say is the best thing about making others feel good through kindness?

When:

1. When does Baanab perform acts of kindness for their little brother and a stranger on the way to school?
2. When does Baanab realise that their actions have made a positive impact on others?

Where:

1. Where does Baanab perform their acts of kindness during the day?
2. Where does Baanab get the feeling of warmth and pride, and who is present at that moment?

Why:

1. Why does Baanab initially wish they could disappear at school? Give some reasons from the story.
2. Why does Baanab's teacher praise the class for their efforts to be kind and for taking part in the kindness challenge?
3. How does this acknowledgement impact Baanab?

ANSWERS

Who:

1. The main character of the story is Baanab.
2. Nana gives Baanab advice about kindness. The advice is to 'Just be kind' because people may not realise how special Baanab is.
3. A. Kind is a local hero. Her note is significant because it shows that Baanab's acts of kindness are recognised and appreciated by others, including someone well known for their kindness.

What:

1. Baanab's teacher announces that the class will be taking part in a kindness hunt. This activity involves looking out for kind actions throughout the

day and earning pebbles for a jar. The person with the most pebbles gets to choose a special activity for the class. This activity is important because it encourages kindness and working together.

2. Some examples of kind acts that Baanab does throughout the day include helping their little brother in the morning, assisting a mother with a pram on the way to school, picking up a dropped coat and helping classmates with tasks like getting pencils and getting a drink for someone who was coughing.
3. Nana says that the best thing about making others feel good through kindness is that it not only makes the person being helped feel good but also brings a warm and proud feeling to the person doing the kind act.

Where:

1. Baanab performs acts of kindness at home, on the way to school and in the classroom.
2. Baanab feels a warm feeling of pride when their classmates acknowledge and appreciate their kind actions during the discussion in the classroom.

When:

1. Baanab performs acts of kindness for their little brother and a stranger on the way to school in the morning.
2. Baanab realises that their actions have made a positive impact on others when their classmates share stories of how Baanab helped them during the kindness challenge.

Why:

1. Baanab initially wishes they could disappear from school because some students would start trouble for no reason and say hurtful things. This made Baanab feel like they weren't valued or noticed by others.
2. Baanab's teacher praises the class for their efforts to be kind and take part in the kindness challenge to encourage positive behaviour and to foster a kind and supportive environment.
3. The praise from Baanab's teacher and classmates makes Baanab feel proud and warm inside because they realise that their kind actions have a meaningful impact on others. This recognition boosts their self-esteem and motivates them to continue being kind.

ACTIVITY

HUNT FOR KINDNESS

As a class, take part in a hunt for kindness. This activity involves looking out for kind actions and earning pebbles for a jar. The person who has contributed the most pebbles gets to choose a special activity for the class. This activity is important because it encourages kindness and working together.

CONCLUSION

In this chapter we looked at how we can use the ideas of superheroes to talk about kindness, compassion and how this leads to allyship. We explored allyship and the idea that fundamentally at its core is kindness. I hope you have enjoyed writing stories with your class in response to the story of Baanab. What did you notice about the story and its characters?

In what ways did I try to encompass the concepts of raising our own awareness around stereotypes, prejudice and assumptions?

What did you reflect on for your own learning?

FURTHER READING AND RESOURCES

Here's why your child's superhero obsession is actually good for them: Four ways to encourage everyday heroics. *Huffpost.* Available at: www.huffingtonpost.co.uk/entry/kids-everyday-hero-not-superhero_uk_5cb5f21de4b0ffefe3b7b233

Ryan North on kindness, comics and the appeal of superheroes, with Elizabeth Oldfield. *Theos.* Available at: www.theosthinktank.co.uk/comment/2021/12/01/ryan-north-on-kindness-comics-and-the-appeal-of-superheroes

Marvel Studios Character Encyclopedia (2024) Updated edition by K. Knox and A. Bray

The DC Comics Encyclopedia (2021) New edition by M. Manning and S. Wiacek

Why do Character Strengths Matter? Available at: www.viacharacter.org/

The Hero with a Thousand Faces by Joseph Campbell

8

WHAT DO YOU NEED? ENCOURAGING CHILDREN TO SPEAK OUT AND STAND WITH OTHERS

KEY CONCEPTS

The key concepts covered in this chapter are:

- empowering children and young people to use their voices to stand up and speak out;
- supporting mental health;
- safeguarding against bullying in schools and other educational settings.

INTRODUCTION

Allyship is the practice of using your voice, power and influence to address the needs of marginalised groups. The opposite of an ally is an opponent. This is someone who opposes or competes with another person or group. In the same way, as we say, an ally can be described as a friend in the moment. An opponent is a foe; rather than supporting or caring for you, they oppose or harm you and engage in bullying behaviour against you. Concerning schools and other educational settings, these individuals bully and make others feel unsafe and unwelcome.

Bullying can take many forms, including physical and verbal, as well as relational. Schools must prevent and respond to bullying behaviour. *Keeping*

Children Safe in Education (KCSIE) (DfE, 2023c) emphasises the importance of having appropriate policies and procedures in place to safeguard and promote children's welfare, including measures to prevent bullying, including cyberbullying, prejudice-based and discriminatory bullying.

Sometimes, people who appear to be friends can also engage in bullying behaviour. This is known as friendship bullying or relational bullying and commonly involves behaviours such as exclusion, manipulation and control.

Friendship bullying is a lot more common than we think, but it can be difficult to identify because it happens in subtle ways. Friendship or relational bullying can be hidden because the person doing the bullying uses their closeness to another person to gain power and control, commonly through emotional manipulation.

Disabled people and other marginalised groups, including care-experienced children, are more likely to be victims of friendship or relational bullying than their peers. Vulnerabilities can lead to people taking advantage of them. Other identified risks include low self-esteem and being part of a group made to feel like outsiders.

Addressing bullying in schools is crucial as it can significantly impact the wellbeing and development of students. Beyond immediate emotional distress, bullying can lead to long-term psychological effects, hindering academic performance and social integration.

Studies show that being bullied in school leads to a higher risk of mental health difficulties and being bullied at work (GOV.UK, 2015).

Allyship plays a pivotal role in combatting bullying by fostering a culture of support, empathy and collective responsibility within our schools and workplaces. Encouraging a community of allies creates a network of support where students and staff feel empowered to speak up, seek help and actively work towards creating a safer, more inclusive environment.

Being an ally is about supporting and standing up for marginalised or oppressed people. Part of this is being willing to show genuine curiosity, empathy and compassion for other people.

To show that we are allies, we must use our collective voices to amplify the voices of others.

One of the most important questions we can ever ask is, 'Are you okay?'

Just those three words can be incredibly powerful. Asking this question is a simple way to demonstrate genuine concern for someone's wellbeing and can open up a space for people to share their feelings, struggles and experiences.

Speaking out against bullying and displaying allyship entails employing words that express support and firm resistance to bullying. Encouraging words like 'Are you okay? I'm here for you.' Provide support for the victim and act as a deterrent to the bully. These words give allies the confidence to stand up and speak out. It also lets the bully and the victim know that their acts are taken seriously and that help is on hand.

But how do you ask if someone is okay, and is it always appropriate? The specific phrases and customs we use for enquiring about wellbeing can differ significantly, but the underlying concern for a person's welfare is a universal human sentiment. Instead of words, we might use gestures, touch or acts of kindness. The terms may differ, but the intention is the same.

Sometimes, people might not feel comfortable opening up immediately, but knowing someone has noticed them makes a significant difference when they are ready. Allyship often requires empathetic understanding and the patience to recognise that our kindness may not immediately lead to someone opening up about their struggles. One of the things we always say about the importance of kindness is that we can't see the challenges someone is dealing with they can be both visible and invisible.

One of the first people I spoke to about my negative experiences leaving headship and the bullying behaviour shown by others was Professor Paul Miller. Professor Miller (PhD) is an Educational Leadership and Social Justice professor who researches anti-racism and social justice in education and educational leadership, particularly regarding staff progression and leadership behaviour.

He said, 'Standing with you.' That, to me, demonstrated true allyship. It showed genuine interest and care.

WHY IS THIS IMPORTANT?

Discrimination's impact on mental health is significant. Encouraging people, especially children, to 'be more resilient' or 'show more grit' oversimplifies the issue. This overlooks the depth of emotional distress and psychological harm caused by discrimination. Emphasising this highlights the need for a more compassionate and supportive approach, acknowledging the real, detrimental effects discrimination can have on mental health. It's essential to create environments that actively combat discrimination rather than solely burdening affected individuals to cope.

Solidarity and support through allyship play a vital role in combatting discrimination's impact on mental health. They involve actively standing with those facing discrimination, offering understanding and support. This approach acknowledges the challenges individuals might face due to discrimination. It's a way to bridge the gap and show that they're not alone in facing these issues, which can significantly improve their wellbeing.

HOW DO WE MODEL STANDING UP AND SPEAKING OUT?

The conversation starters we can use to show that we are willing to stand with someone and demonstrate allyship are the same ones we can use to support mental health.

From September 2020, the mandatory health education curriculum teaches pupils about mental health and wellbeing as part of health and relationships education. At primary age, pupils learn that mental wellbeing is a normal part of daily life and why self-care is important.

Also, in England, the DfE offered a grant for schools to train a senior mental health lead, to develop and implement a whole-school approach to mental health and wellbeing by 2025.

If you are not a trained mental health first aider, I would encourage you to become one. Mental health first aid (MHFA) courses teach participants how to recognise, understand and support someone who could be dealing with a mental health problem. The goal of the training is to give you the knowledge, tools and abilities to identify common mental health issues and to offer early support and assistance to someone going through a mental health crisis.

My friend, Louise Larkum, owns and directs Mindcare Training, which provides wellbeing training to promote positive mental health and is an accredited MHFA course provider. Lou put me on her MHFA training course because she recognised that I was feeling low then and could use the training to support myself and help others.

Some of the key questions/phrases I learnt are:

1. How are you feeling? I can see; I noticed that ...
2. Is there anything you'd like to talk about? I know that ...
3. I'm here if you ever need to talk. Let's arrange to meet ...
4. What can I do to help you? Who can I contact?

5. What support do you have? I can recommend ...
6. Would you like to tell me more about your experiences? That sounds ...
7. Tell me about what happened. I'm here to listen ...
8. What do you need from me? How can I help?

PAUSE FOR SELF-REFLECTION

Consider this list of questions I learnt on the MHFA training course.

- What would you add?
- Who are your allies?
- Who asks if you're okay?

If we are trying to encourage children to stand up and speak out for others, we must show our commitment to change our own behaviour by reflecting on whether we display any bullying behaviours. Bullying behaviour by educators not only affects students directly but also sets a harmful example that contradicts the values schools aim to instil.

Reflect on whether you do any of the following:

1. *verbal aggression*: using harsh language, shouting, or making demeaning remarks;
2. *exclusion or favouritism*: intentionally ignoring certain students or showing favouritism towards others;
3. *public shaming or humiliation*: telling off a student in front of their peers, ridiculing or embarrassing;
4. *power imbalance*: using your authority to intimidate, threaten, or manipulate students rather than guiding or supporting them;
5. *ignoring or dismissing concerns*: brushing off or dismissing a student's complaints of bullying or not taking their concerns seriously (because you have decided that you don't believe them) or think their complaint is serious enough.

I'm not saying that you're intentionally engaging in bullying behaviour; I don't know you personally – but it's something to reflect on. We would not accept this behaviour from adults towards us, so it is important to call this out when we see our colleagues showing this behaviour towards our students. If we encourage children to speak out and stand with others, we must show our commitment to supporting individuals facing discrimination through our own demonstration of allyship and empathy.

How can we do this through our own actions and behaviours?

- *Solidarity through action.* Active listening stands as a pivotal practice. When individuals from underrepresented groups speak, offering undivided attention is crucial, avoiding interruptions and truly comprehending their perspective.
- *Amplifying voices.* Encouraging and acknowledging the ideas and contributions of marginalised individuals is another significant aspect. Giving credit and support uplifts their voices.
- *Educational endeavours.* Taking the initiative to educate ourselves about underrepresented groups' experiences, challenges and histories is essential. Reading, attending workshops and actively seeking information are impactful steps.
- *Advocacy and speaking out.* Using privilege to speak out against discrimination, bias, or micro-aggressions is critical. It's an opportunity to educate others and challenge unfair practices.
- *Self-reflection and bias check.* As mentioned, reflecting on personal biases and actively working to address and change them is fundamental. Acknowledge that recognising and challenging biases is an ongoing process.
- *Collaborative endeavours.* Collaborating with others and listening to diverse perspectives is powerful. It demonstrates that everyone's voice will be heard and respected.
- *Continuous learning and growth.* The best thing about being an educator is the opportunity to educate and re-educate yourself continuously. Continuous self-improvement allows you to assess your allyship efforts regularly; being receptive to feedback and adapting the approach as needed is key to continually improving support for those facing discrimination.

The journey of allyship and empathy is both a collective and an individual endeavour. Acknowledging the power of continual learning and growth, particularly as educators, reinforces the importance of continuous self-improvement. This is an important message to share with our pupils.

HOW DO WE TEACH IT?

Teaching allyship and empathy to children involves fostering a culture of respect, understanding and action. Start by modelling these values through your own behaviour and interactions with your students, colleagues and parents/carers.

The Anti-Bullying Alliance (ABA) is a coalition of organisations and individuals united against bullying. One of the focal areas within ABA's resources is addressing friendship-based or relational bullying, often termed 'false friendships'. Recognising these complex dynamics among children can be hard for adults and educators.

The ABA offers guidance which emphasises the importance of discussing with children the essence of genuine friendship. A significant concern arises when individuals experience bullying from someone they believe to be a friend, amplifying the emotional impact. Therefore, educating children about the traits of a good friend is crucial. Its two main recommendations are:

1. talk to children about what it is to be a good friend;
2. talk to children about the difference between banter and bullying.

(Anti-Bullying Alliance, n.d.)

A good friend consistently checks in on your wellbeing, offers support and actively listens when you're distressed. Understanding the difference between banter and bullying is to distinguish between playful teasing and hurtful behaviour. Understanding this difference empowers children and young people to establish boundaries and ensure they feel safe while interacting with their peers.

Extending empathy for bullies is challenging but crucial to addressing and potentially mitigating their behaviour. Recognising that their conduct might stem from a lack of positive attention, feelings of powerlessness, or even being subjected to bullying in other environments can help cultivate empathy. Including every class member in group discussions and activities without judgement can help bullies learn healthier ways to deal with their emotions and conflicts, thereby potentially reducing instances of bullying. Empathy for bullies doesn't excuse their actions; it seeks to understand and address the underlying issues that drive their behaviour.

KEY QUESTIONS

Incorporating key questions can spark meaningful discussions and critical thinking among children.

1. What does it mean to be a good friend and supporter to everyone?
2. Can you think of a time when someone stood up for you or someone else? How did that make you feel?
3. How do you ask your friends if they are okay?
4. Why is listening important when someone shares their experiences or feelings?
5. How can we ensure everyone feels included and respected in our classroom or community?
6. What can we do when seeing someone treated unfairly or unkindly?
7. How can understanding different perspectives help us in our daily lives?
8. How can we learn more about different cultures, backgrounds and experiences?
9. Why is it important to keep learning and growing as a person?

These questions can stimulate conversations that encourage empathy, inclusivity and understanding among children, prompting them to reflect on their actions and the impact they can have on others. In addition, the DfE have developed practical materials for primary and secondary schools to train staff about teaching mental wellbeing (DfE, 2021b).

LESSON OR CLASSROOM ACTIVITIES

Setting clear ground rules is essential for fostering a positive learning environment, particularly when it comes to protecting students' safety and wellbeing. Establishing clear guidelines helps teachers to create an environment where students feel safe, respected and empowered to take an active role.

These rules can include a wide range of topics, such as social relations, physical limits, mental health and wellbeing. These are important conversations.

Establishing clear guidelines is crucial to creating a supportive learning atmosphere, especially when it comes to safeguarding the health and safety of our pupils. These guidelines emphasise the value of everyone's safety by establishing common understanding of appropriate behaviour which enhances emotional safety.

EXAMPLE GROUND RULES

(Taken from DfE, 2020)

Respect privacy. We can discuss examples but don't use names or descriptions identifying anyone, including ourselves. We never put anyone 'on the spot'.

Listen to others. It's okay to challenge a view or disagree, but we listen properly before making assumptions or deciding how to respond. Everyone has the right to feel listened to.

No judgement. We can explore beliefs and misunderstandings about a topic without fear of judgement.

Right to pass. Every pupil has the right to choose not to answer a question or join the discussion if a topic makes them uncomfortable.

ACTIVITY

REFLECTING ON THE PAST TO IMPROVE THE FUTURE

OBJECTIVE

This activity is designed to prompt reflection on past situations where someone was a victim. It encourages participants to recall what occurred to the victim, how bystanders reacted and what the allies (individuals who actively supported the victim) did. The goal is to foster an understanding of people's roles in such situations and encourage brainstorming about future actions to help victims effectively.

Relating this to asking each other if we are okay involves drawing parallels between the victim's experience and the need for support in everyday interactions. By exploring what bystanders and allies did in the past, the activity prompts individuals to consider their responses when someone might need help or support.

In discussing what the allies could do next time to ensure the victim is okay, the activity encourages proactive thinking about supportive actions. This aspect directly connects to checking in with others to ensure their wellbeing and considering strategies to offer meaningful support. It's about learning from past situations to improve future responses and create a safer, more supportive environment for everyone.

EQUIPMENT

- Paper or journals: to write or draw their responses to the questions about past situations involving victims, bystanders and allies.
- Pens, pencils, or colouring materials: write down thoughts, draw, or illustrate ideas related to the activity.
- A whiteboard or flipchart (optional): working with a group, this can be used to note down key points or responses for everyone to see.
- Markers or chalk (if using a board): for writing or drawing to illustrate key points during the discussion.
- Simple symbols or drawings: depending on the age group, you might consider using some props or visual aids to help illustrate the roles of victims, bystanders and allies.

Remember, the main focus is discussion and reflection, so the emphasis is more on engaging participants in conversation and thought rather than relying heavily on equipment or materials.

INSTRUCTIONS

To begin this exercise, talk about the roles that allies, bystanders and victims play in stories and how, unfortunately, similar dynamics also happen in real-life situations. After having a general conversation about it, you can then focus on the effects that being in one of these roles can have. This prepares students for the next exercise, which allows them to investigate these roles in more detail in relation to reflecting on actual situations.

Victims, bystanders and allies are normal characters we read about in stories, but, unfortunately, instead of being a story, it might be about things that happen in real life.

A *victim* is hurt, treated unfairly, or upset about something that has happened. Just like in stories, they're the ones who need help or support because something hasn't been right or fair.

A *bully* is an individual (or group of people) who repeatedly behaves unkindly or aggressively towards others, trying to make them feel scared, sad, or powerless. Bullies might use unkind words, exclude others, or even physically hurt them. Sometimes bullies do this because they don't feel good about themselves or are being bullied by others.

Bystanders are the people who are around when something happens. They might see or hear what's happening to the person who feels hurt or upset. Sometimes, they might not know what to do, so they watch or stay quiet.

Allies are the heroes in the story. They are the ones who see when something isn't fair or when someone needs help, and they take action to make things better. They stand up for the person who is feeling upset or treated unfairly. They might comfort them, find someone who can help, or speak up to make things fair. By understanding these roles, you learn the important part you might play in different situations. You learn that being an ally – the one who helps – is a powerful and kind role to play.

KEY QUESTIONS

Think of a time when someone was a victim. (Don't name anyone.)

- What happened to the victim?
- What did the bystanders do?
- What did the allies do?
- What could the allies do next time to ensure the victim is okay?

Give each pupil time to give feedback to the class on what they have written/ drawn. By the end of the activity, pupils should have gained a deeper understanding of the roles of victims, bystanders and allies in different situations. Ideally, they should have learnt:

1. *understanding of roles*: recognising the different roles when someone is hurt or treated unfairly. This includes understanding the impact each role can have on the outcome;
2. *empathy and support*: cultivating empathy towards victims and understanding the importance of offering support in such situations;
3. *responsibility*: acknowledging the responsibility of bystanders and the impact their actions (or inaction) can have on the situation;
4. *empowerment*: encouragement to be an ally, understanding that positive action can make a difference and create a more supportive environment;
5. *reflection for improvement*: reflecting on past experiences to consider how allies could act differently in the future to support victims better. This involves critical thinking about what actions we should take to ensure the wellbeing of those in need.

HOW TO ASK THE VICTIM IF THEY'RE OKAY

After you have discussed the concepts of allies, victims and bystanders, go on to discuss how to ask victims if they are okay.

This involves guiding them through showing care and support while respecting the other person's feelings.

GUIDED APPROACH

1. *Understanding feelings*: start by explaining different emotions and feelings. Children must understand that sometimes people feel sad, upset, or uncomfortable.

2. *Approach with care*: teach them to approach someone who seems upset or hurt with gentleness and kindness. Please encourage them to use a soft tone of voice and considerate body language.
3. *Ask open-ended questions*: encourage them to ask open-ended questions like, 'How can I help?' or 'What do you need?' Give the person space to share if they feel comfortable. Agree on key phrases, signs and gestures you can use as a class to check on each other.
4. *Active listening*: teach children to listen actively. This means giving their full attention, making eye contact if they feel comfortable and taking turns when speaking or using agreed symbols. Encourage them to show empathy by saying things like, 'That doesn't seem kind' or 'I'm here for you.'
5. *Respect boundaries*: explain the importance of respecting boundaries. If the person doesn't want to talk, teach children to say, 'Okay, I'm here when you're ready.'
6. *Getting help*: emphasise that if the situation seems serious or the person is in danger, it's essential to seek help from a trusted adult.

Emphasise that offering support is about caring and respect, and it's okay if the person doesn't want to talk. It's about showing that you care and are there for them if they need it.

ROLE PLAY OR DRAWINGS

Role plays and drawings can be powerful tools to help children understand and practice asking someone if they're okay.

ROLE PLAY

1. *Set the scene*: create simple scenarios where one child acts as someone who might be upset and the other child takes on the role of the supportive friend.
2. *Guidance*: before starting, guide how to approach the 'upset' friend carefully, ask open-ended questions, listen actively and respect boundaries.
3. *Switch roles*: have the children switch roles after the first scenario. This helps both understand how it feels to be the supportive friend and the one needing support.

DRAWINGS

1. *Prompt with scenarios*: ask children to draw a scenario where someone might be upset or need help. This could be someone sitting alone if they normally play with others or don't seem their usual self.
2. *Encourage expression*: ask them to draw what they would do to help. This could include speech bubbles with kind words or actions they would take to offer support.

Display these in the classroom as a reminder. Even better, ask children to assemble for the rest of the school/parents, guardians and carers to show what they have been learning and why.

After the activities, discussing what they learnt and how they felt during the role play or drawing exercise is essential.

SAFEGUARDING: TALKING AND GETTING SUPPORT

(Taken from DfE, 2020)

Remind younger pupils to talk to a trusted adult when:

- they are experiencing friendship problems;
- they feel lonely.

Check that older pupils:

- can describe what loneliness is;
- know that it can help to talk about feelings;
- are aware of the adults they can talk to;
- can suggest actions a character might take if they were lonely (structured scenario).

CONCLUSION

This chapter focused on empowering children to speak out and stand in solidarity with others. We discussed the importance of encouraging empathy and support for those facing challenges or feeling upset. The chapter teaches children to recognise when someone needs help, approach the situation carefully, ask open-ended questions, listen actively and respect boundaries. Role playing scenarios and drawing activities are suggested to help children understand and practice offering support. We discussed mental health and bullying – in particular, the importance of recognising and supporting individuals who might be experiencing emotional distress or challenges. Encouraging children to ask if someone is okay nurtures an environment where mental health concerns can be acknowledged and addressed. It fosters a culture of open communication and support, which is essential in promoting positive mental wellbeing. This proactive approach to caring for others' emotional wellbeing contributes significantly to creating a supportive and understanding school community. By teaching children simple ways to be attentive and empathetic towards others' emotions individually, we ensure they all feel more comfortable seeking or offering help when needed.

FURTHER READING AND RESOURCES

Promoting Children and Young People's Mental Health and Wellbeing: A Whole School or College Approach (2021) Public Health England, working with the Department for Education. Available at: https://assets.publishing.service.gov.uk/media/614cc965d3bf7f718518029c/Promoting_children_and_young_people_s_mental_health_and_wellbeing.pdf

NSPCC Learning (2024) *How to have Difficult Conversations with Children.* Available at: https://learning.nspcc.org.uk/safeguarding-child-protection/how-to-have-difficult-conversations-with-children

Anti-Bullying Alliance (n.d.) *10 Key Principles.* Available at: https://anti-bullyingalliance.org.uk/tools-information/all-about-bullying/preventing-bullying/10-key-principles

NHS (2022) *Talking to Your Child About Feelings*. Available at: www.nhs.uk/mental-health/children-and-young-adults/advice-for-parents/talk-to-children-about-feelings/

NSPCC Learning (n.d.) *Speak Out Stay Safe*. Available at: https://learning.nspcc.org.uk/services/speak-out-stay-safe

MHFA (n.d.) Resources for schools. Available at: https://mhfaengland.org/mhfa-centre/resources/for-schools/

9

LEARNING FROM THE PAST

KEY CONCEPTS

The key concepts covered in this chapter are:

- different forms of discrimination;
- ways in which we might discriminate in the classroom;
- the importance of names and their meanings;
- the importance of learning lessons from history so that we don't repeat our mistakes.

INTRODUCTION

'If I have seen further, it is by standing on the shoulders of giants.'

The phrase is often credited to Sir Isaac Newton, who wrote it in a letter to his rival Robert Hooke in 1676. Since then, it has been used to describe the idea that knowledge is cumulative, and that each generation builds upon the work of those who came before them.

This chapter will explore how advocates and allies who came before us can inspire us to improve the present and fight for a better future for our children.

My heritage is from Ghana in West Africa. We have a traditional symbol system called *adinkra*. This consists of simple pictorial representations of proverbs and metaphors. As an artist, I wanted to design my own adinkra-type symbol to honour my ancestry but also represent hope for the future. I drew a rough sketch and sent it to a designer in Ghana. It is a symbol that represents 'Collective knowledge and understanding' (you can see this on my blog site (Akinde, 2023).

Both the metaphor at the beginning of this chapter and my symbol remind us that it is important to recognise that knowledge is collective. It is an ongoing collaboration, with each generation advancing due to the groundwork laid by their predecessors – a reminder that our growth and innovation are deeply rooted in the collective heritage of human knowledge.

KEY HISTORICAL EVENTS TO LEARN FROM

History offers a wealth of lessons on the powerful impact of allyship as a way to stand up to discrimination. It also teaches us the consequences of remaining passive in the face of injustice. Sadly, we still seem to be repeating history. We can see this through the injustices we see worldwide today.

By examining different forms of historical discrimination and if they were eliminated, we can grasp the strategies that worked, the mistakes that hindered progress and the pivotal roles of allies and bystanders.

Let's go on to look at some common historical areas of discrimination in more detail.

RACIAL DISCRIMINATION

Slavery: The transatlantic slave trade involved the forced migration and enslavement of millions of Africans. The brutality this displacement caused still shows up in disparities and discrimination seen today. Regrettably, modern slavery persists, echoing the injustices of the past.

Apartheid in South Africa: This was the systematic racial segregation of and discrimination against non-white South Africans. Although it officially ended in the early 1990s, segregated housing patterns and economic disparities still exist along racial lines, and unequal access to quality education and healthcare continues to affect non-white communities.

Jim Crow Laws in the US: This was legalised segregation that marginalised African Americans in public facilities, education and housing, barring them from using the same facilities as white Americans. Its impact is still visible today, particularly through systemic issues within the criminal justice system that disproportionately affect African American communities.

The Windrush Scandal: This unfolded in the mid-2010s and brought to life the mistreatment of Caribbean immigrants to Britain, the 'Windrush generation', by the UK government, resulting in wrongful detentions and deportations.

Genocide: Rooted in discrimination, genocides are acts that aim to wipe out a national, ethnic, or religious group. These acts are driven by pure hatred. One of the largest and most notable genocides was the holocaust, which led to the murder of 6 million Jewish people. The Nazis also targeted Romani and other marginalised communities.

RAISING AWARENESS

In 1969, the United Nations (UN) Convention on the Elimination of Racial Discrimination came into force. Independent experts monitor the implementation of its core purpose, 'to take action against the injustice of racial discrimination and the danger it represents' (McDougall, 2021).

It states, 'Racial discrimination remains a barrier to the full realisation of human rights.' However, it also acknowledges that 'Despite progress in some areas, exclusions and restrictions based on race, colour, descent, national or ethnic origin continue to cause conflict, suffering and loss of life' (UN, 1965).

There are 177 nation-states signed up for this; they are monitored through regular reports by the committee, which issues concrete recommendations on how various forms of racism can be eliminated. As they say, people can't live a full life if they are discriminated against because of their race.

GENDER DISCRIMINATION

Gender pay gap: Women historically faced (and still face) unequal pay compared to men for the same work.

The suffragette movement: This highlighted women's struggle for voting rights in the early 20th century. The movement was predominately led by and, therefore, focused on white women. Black women, Native American and other marginalised women were often excluded from the rights the movement sought.

Sexual harassment and violence: Historically, women are at higher risk of experiencing unwanted sexual advances, domestic violence and sexual assault. Despite increased advocacy and more societal condemnation, issues such as gender-based violence still persist.

Education: In ancient civilisations, such as ancient Greece and medieval Europe, education was restricted to just boys and men. When women and girls were allowed to attend school, this was heavily restricted. In many countries, women and girls are still being given limited and unequal access to education or denied any right to education at all. We can see this in regions under Taliban rule, where, during their rule in Afghanistan in the late 1990s, they imposed a complete ban on education for girls beyond the age of eight.

Arranged marriages without consent: Historically, arranged marriages happened at a very young age for girls, sometimes in childhood. They were often arranged for familial, economic or cultural reasons without asking the people involved, but now we value consent and some choices regarding these have evolved.

RAISING AWARENESS

Addressing gender inequalities is still paramount. The International Day of the Girl Child, celebrated annually on 11 October, was established by the UN General Assembly in 2011 to highlight the challenges girls face and promote their empowerment and human rights. It's dedicated to shedding light on the unique obstacles girls encounter, including limited education access, gender-based violence and discrimination, while supporting initiatives that enhance their wellbeing and success.

DISCRIMINATION BASED ON LGBTQI+ IDENTITY

LGBTQI+ rights: Same-sex relationships are still illegal in many countries, leading to persecution and imprisonment.

Section 28: Legislation that prohibited the 'promotion' of homosexuality by local authorities in the late 1980s and early 1990s stated that a local authority 'shall not intentionally promote homosexuality or publish material with the intention of promoting homosexuality' or 'promote the teaching in any maintained school of the acceptability of homosexuality as a pretended family relationship' (Section 2A). It was eventually repealed in 2003 in Scotland and 2000 in the rest of the UK.

Medical pathologising: The medical community historically classified homosexuality as a mental disorder, leading to treatments and therapies that aimed to 'cure' individuals.

Misgendering: Purposely using a person's incorrect gender identity or pronouns even after being corrected.

Social stigmatisation: Social stigma leads to ostracisation, rejection by families and societal discrimination.

Violence and hate crimes: Targeted violence, hate crimes and even murder due to sexual orientation or gender identity. Rates of violence and hate crimes are highest towards trans people.

RAISING AWARENESS

As per the findings of the government's 2017 *National LGBT Survey* (GEO, 2018), among those who were in school from 2016–17, one-third reported that they encountered hostility because they identified as LGBT or because others thought they did. The uninvited disclosure of one's LGBT status (which happened to 21 per cent of respondents) commonly resulted in verbal harassment (19 per cent). Others claimed they were left out of activities or gatherings (6 per cent). A few had been subjected to physical (2 per cent) and/or sexual harassment (also 2 per cent).

In school,

- 64 per cent of young trans people, 35 per cent of young bisexual people and 57 per cent of young non-binary people were bullied for their LGBT+ identity; 64 per cent of LGBT+ people have experienced anti-LGBT+ violence or abuse (Hubbard, 2021);
- half of LGBT+ students hear homophobic slurs 'frequently' or 'often' (Stonewall, 2017);
- LGBT+ students are three times more likely to self-harm (Just Like Us, 2021).

These results support a 2013 study by Robinson et al. that indicated bullying against LGBTQI youth occurs twice as frequently in secondary schools as it does for heterosexual youth. In general, as people progressed from secondary school to college and eventually university, the prevalence of events decreased.

Other pupils were the ones who committed the most significant incidents most frequently according to the responders (in 88 per cent of cases). However, teaching staff members were responsible for nearly a tenth (9 per cent) of the crimes. Since 83 per cent of these occurrences go unreported, it's critical that we increase awareness of this.

RELIGIOUS DISCRIMINATION

The Crusades: These religious wars from the 11th to 13th centuries were driven by religious fervour, resulting in the persecution and forced conversion of non-Christians in regions like the Middle East.

The Holocaust: The systematic extermination of 6 million Jewish people by the Nazis during World War II.

The Partition of India: The division of India into India and Pakistan in 1947 led to violence and displacement between Hindus, Muslims and Sikhs based on religious differences.

The Spanish Inquisition: Initiated in the late 15th century, it targeted Jews, Muslims and others who were perceived as heretics by the Catholic Church. They faced persecution, expulsion, or execution if they did not convert.

Northern Ireland Troubles: Deep-seated religious and political conflict between Catholic nationalists and Protestant unionists in Northern Ireland.

RAISING AWARENESS

These historical instances of religious discrimination make it painfully evident that the human experience has been marred by acts of cruelty and intolerance. Sadly, we can see many current examples of persecution, stigmatisation and genocide still going on today, casting a shadow across the globe. Conflicts around the world are still being fuelled by longstanding historical grievances or modern geopolitical tensions. Current conflicts across Europe, Africa, the Middle East and both South and Southeast Asia show us that, regrettably, we are still learning how to co-exist and respect all religions, faiths and beliefs.

DISCRIMINATION BASED ON DISABILITY

Forced sterilisation: In the early 20th century, various countries, including the United States and several European nations, implemented eugenic policies that forcibly sterilised individuals with disabilities to prevent them from reproducing, under the belief that their genes were inferior.

Institutionalisation and isolation: Historically, institutions like asylums and 'homes' for people with disabilities were widespread. These places often provided inadequate care, isolation from society and sometimes even abusive treatment.

Lack of access to education: Historically many individuals with disabilities were denied access to education. For instance, in the UK, the 1880 Education Act explicitly excluded children 'unsuitable for ordinary schools', often encompassing those with disabilities.

Inhumane treatments: Before the development of modern medicine and ethics, people with disabilities were subjected to inhuman treatments, such as electroshock therapy, lobotomies and other experimental procedures, often without consent.

Employment discrimination: Historically individuals with disabilities were frequently excluded from the workforce and deemed incapable of performing tasks despite their abilities. This led to economic marginalisation and dependency on caregivers. Disabled people are more likely to face abuse by primary caregivers due to the vulnerabilities that can occur as a result of their disabilities.

RAISING AWARENESS

Our history of inhumane treatment, dehumanisation and exclusion of people with disabilities is something that disabled people and their allies are increasingly united against. Disability History Month UK, which is celebrated from 16 November to 16 December, is an opportunity to recognise and promote disability history, and to celebrate the lives and achievements of disabled people. Now, due to advancements in inclusive education and improved accessibility, the emphasis for the future is on creating an inclusive environment and equal opportunities for all. Thus moving away from the medical mode, which views disability as a problem to be fixed and more towards the medical model that focus on societal barriers and the need to adapt environments for inclusivity.

Across all areas, while progress has been made, inequities still persist today. Although we have highlighted a few of them here, we should also consider other forms of discrimination that have gained more attention in more recent years, such as:

- **cultural appropriation:** this occurs when elements of one culture are adopted or used by individuals from another culture without understanding or respecting the significance or history behind those elements. It can perpetuate stereotypes and undermine the cultural integrity of the originating group;
- **ableism:** this is the belief that 'abled' individuals are superior. It manifests in attitudes, policies and societal structures that exclude or limit the opportunities for people with disabilities, such as employment discrimination (by failing to make reasonable adjustments) or the lack of accessible public spaces;
- **colourism:** discrimination within a particular ethnic or racial community based on the shade of skin colour. Lighter skin tones are sometimes favoured over darker ones, leading to biases in areas like employment, relationships, societal treatment and the use of illegal skin-lightening creams;
- **linguistic discrimination:** individuals are discriminated against based on their accent, dialect, or language proficiency. It can affect opportunities in education, employment and social acceptance.

PAUSE FOR SELF-REFLECTION

Take a moment to consider your awareness of historical discrimination and how it has shaped your perspective. Has your understanding changed from what you have learnt in this chapter?

Reflect on how you have incorporated the lessons from historical discrimination into your teaching, if at all. Have you highlighted these issues in your curriculum? Do you encourage discussions about discrimination, bias and inequality?

Think about your classroom environment. Do you believe it is inclusive and welcoming to students from all backgrounds? Can you make any further changes or improvements to ensure a more equitable and diverse learning space?

What actions can you take to ensure that the lessons of historical discrimination are actively integrated into your teaching and classroom environment? How can you empower your students to be aware, empathetic and engaged in building a better school environment where bias and discrimination do not exist?

WAYS IN WHICH WE MAY DISCRIMINATE IN THE CLASSROOM

WHAT'S IN A NAME?

Today, it is better understood how important it is to respect people's names. Recently, I did a series of interviews for a news story and, throughout the day, every presenter took the time to learn how to pronounce all the names mentioned accurately. This showed a great deal of respect.

Every name and its cultural heritage deserve acknowledgement and respect. It is not acceptable to refuse to attempt to pronounce someone's name correctly, to shorten or change someone's name to something that's easier for us to learn and say.

Name-related discrimination is a more covert kind of prejudice that pupils and staff can experience at school. Biases against specific names because of cultural or racial distinctions have historically frequently resulted in discrimination and disrespect.

Slave owners frequently ignored their slaves' names, renaming them as they pleased, therefore deliberately robbing them of their identities and cultural ties. By attempting to exercise dominance and control, this act served to further dehumanise them and erase their uniqueness and cultural history. Names were frequently enforced by slave masters as a show of power. They gave people names that had nothing to do with their background or sense of self, such as Tom, Jack, or Sarah. The distinct cultural backgrounds and individual histories of the enslaved were erased when these names were selected purely for the convenience of the slave owners.

Consider: What does your name mean? Is it a name that people may see as unusual?

Have you been in situations where people have struggled to pronounce your name so just didn't attempt to say it correctly? Worse still, have people attempted to change your name to make it easier for them to pronounce?

In live television interviews, both in January 2022 and again in May 2023, Dr Shola Mos Shogbamimu, a British-Nigerian lawyer, academic and activist, repeatedly had to ask a presenter to say her surname correctly after they struggled to pronounce it (Vassell, 2023). In response, one viewer stated: 'I get my surname pronounced wrong all the time. As a kid I let it go, now I correct people. It's my name, say it properly.'

As someone with dyslexia, I often struggle with word pronunciation and spelling things out phonetically, but I would not use this as an excuse for disrespecting someone's name and therefore their identity. The reaction to Dr Shogbamimu's stance, that she would not move on with the interview until the presenter said her name correctly, reiterated to people how important this was. It may have appeared to be a simple point, but it was important.

My full name is Frances Emma Abla Akinde née Datson.

Frances is French and means 'free' or, more precisely, 'a free woman from France'. People often misspell it as Francis with an I. This leads to them mistaking my gender. I have even had people question why my parents gave me what they perceive to be a man's name.

My first middle name is *Emma* because my dad's name is Emmanuel.

My second name is *Abla*; it is from the Ewe people of Ghana and means Tuesday born. This is an important tradition in Ghana, where every child is named after the day they were born. The only exception to this is twins or multiple births, where babies are named after their birth order. I have twin boys. My children are of mixed Ghanaian and Nigerian heritage, so their Yoruba names are Taiwo and Kehinde, and their Ewe names are Tse and Atsu. In both cultures, this literally means twin one and twin two.

My surname is *Akinde* (by marriage). It is from the Yoruba tribe in Nigeria and means 'mighty king/warrior has arrived'.

My maiden name is *Datson*. It means son of Datusi. My dad changed it from Datusi when he came to England in the 1970s. It is common, in English, to add the suffixes, son/s/kin/kins/ken at the end of a name.

Getting your pupil's names right matters. Names are a huge part of our identity, culture and history. A name isn't just a label; it reflects who we are, so respecting it is important. Whether it's a name passed down through generations or with a special meaning, it holds pride and history.

Our names are used to define us and our identity. Despite this, name-based discrimination is a common but often overlooked form of bias. When names are mispronounced or misspelt, it sends a hurtful message to a child and their families that their name doesn't matter and that they are not worthy of equal respect.

Because of their names, which may be interpreted as 'foreign', culturally distinctive, or connected to a specific race, religion, or socioeconomic class, people may experience unjust treatment or bias. Discrimination of this kind can occur in a variety of contexts, such as workplaces and educational settings.

For instance, when names are too difficult for students to pronounce, school personnel may abbreviate or alter the names of their students. Instead of enquiring and making an effort to learn how to pronounce a student's name correctly, teachers have been known to modify that student's name. In my own experience, one of my children had his name spelt incorrectly, and the teacher was reluctant to change it because she said it was 'too much hassle'. She protested that she had already laminated his name peg, equipment tray and labelled his book.

Job applicants with names that are perceived as non-traditional or ethnically distinct might face bias during the hiring process, potentially leading to fewer interview opportunities. In schools, students with unique names might be subject to teasing or ridicule from their peers. In addition, people may feel pressured to change their names in order to blend in or escape prejudice, which could have an effect on their sense of self and cultural background.

Deadnaming

We are used to people choosing to rename themselves due to marriage and civil partnerships, but an individual may also feel the need to change their name for other reasons. An artist will often use a stage name, or a writer a nom de plume, to make their name more distinctive or recognisable. A person might feel the need to detach themselves from a complex history caused by trauma, adoption or abuse. Someone might want to reclaim their history, to use a new name to mark the start of a new life, or simply change their name to something they like better.

If I could have any name it would be Sunshine because I love the sun and my surname would be Datusi because it would reinstate my family name. If I wanted to change it by deed poll, I could. I would be able to do that in this country.

The point is that's your choice. Only your birth mother has the legal right to name you when you're born, but you have the right to choose your name and your identity as you grow into it, and it is important to respect everyone's choice of name and refer to them and address them as they prefer. *Deadnaming* specifically relates to referring to a trans or non-binary person by the name they used before transitioning. Deadnaming might be unintentional, but if someone continues to do so after being corrected, that is hurtful and disrespectful. It could be interpreted as a malicious attempt to consciously reject, make fun of, or invalidate someone's gender identity.

Recently, the DfE published draft guidance for schools around their general duties to allow children to change their gender identity (DfE, 2023d). Pupils changing the name they are 'known as' in school has been in the news for a long time – in particular, recently after the tragic murder of Brianna Ghey in February 2023 (see Further reading).

The reporting on the media after her death sparked debate over the right of transgender individuals to decide what name they are called, what pronouns they use and the right to have their wishes respected. Some reports insisted on using Brianna's birth name, and deliberately misgendered her, even after they were advised to correct it. There were also concerns that her death certificate would state the gender assigned at birth, a practice known as *misgendering*.

Schools are advised that if a pupil changes their name legally, they should use that name on their school records. The government issued non-statutory guidance around this after concerns over whether schools should inform parents/carers of a child's wishes (see Further reading).

When one of my sons started secondary school, he decided that he wanted to be known by his middle name and not by his first name. His school rang me to check that this was okay, but explained that they could not change his official records. That was fine by me, but if it wasn't, would my rights as his birth mother take precedent over his rights to have his chosen identity respected? Generally, schools aim to balance the rights of parents/carers and the rights of the child, but if I had objected to the change or if there was a conflict between his rights and mine, how we resolved this would depend on legal and educational policies. This varies depending on the policy of the school; it has been raised that the government's recent guidance may be open to legal challenge, but, overall, as parents/carers and educators, we should all acknowledge a child's evolving autonomy and the importance of respecting their chosen identity. We can't expect children and young people to respect each other if we don't model this to them.

HOW DO WE MODEL IT?

Modelling a commitment to addressing historical discrimination and promoting equity and inclusivity to your students is a powerful way to inspire them to do the same. As educators, it's our role to encourage children and young people to question historical societal norms and expectations. Share examples of when you have made mistakes; this could be bad habits you have changed or opinions you have learnt are wrong. Explain that, in the past, people did things that we now know are wrong; they treated people differently or worse than others. Now, we know that it is important to treat people the same. Over time, we've learnt that no one is better than someone else and to think so is hurtful and unfair.

There are lots of things that we thought were okay in the past that now we've changed our thinking about. Here are some examples, but feel free to add some others. Just ensure that the examples you give around old-fashioned views are culturally and religiously sensitive.

Some examples are:

- *corporal punishment*: we now know that hurting children to make them behave is wrong;
- *foot binding*: girls' feet were deliberately hurt by binding to make them small, which is now understood as a painful and harmful practice;
- *child labour*: children worked in jobs that were not safe or fair, but we now have laws in place to protect a child's right to learn and grow. Unfortunately, we know that this isn't the case across the world, but, as we raise more awareness of this, we can take more action to change things.

HOW DO WE TEACH IT?

Encouraging your students to share their name's origin and meaning fosters respect and inclusion. Practise saying their names, seek help from others, use pronunciation guides, or ask students to share recordings of their names. Let students know you're committed to learning and remembering their names. Encourage them to correct any mistakes, thanking them for guiding you.

Avoid labelling names as 'difficult' or 'unique'. If you have a personal story about a name or someone with the same name, do not make sweeping judgements about people's characters based on their names.

PAUSE FOR REFLECTION

To prepare for discussions in the classroom, take a moment to consider the following.

- Why is it important to treat people the same?
- What have we all got in common?

LESSON OR CLASSROOM ACTIVITY

The following activity encourages self-reflection and research. It also focuses on fostering a sense of respect and appreciation for different cultures. It allows children to explore their own identities.

ACTIVITY

WHAT DOES MY NAME MEAN?

OBJECTIVE

This activity is designed to encourage self-reflection and research, but also foster a sense of respect, appreciation of different cultures and understanding within the classroom. It allows students to explore their identities while learning about the meanings and history of their classmates and their names.

Name analysis activity: Exploring the meanings behind our names is important in understanding cultural diversity and personal identity. This activity encourages students to appreciate the richness of different cultural backgrounds within their classroom. By researching and sharing the significance of their names, students not only gain insight into their peers' diverse heritages, but also develop empathy and respect for each other's unique identities.

Pre-work: For homework, ask students to research the meaning and origins of their name. They can use online name databases, baby name books, or family members' insights. Encourage them to find the cultural, historical, or symbolic significance associated with their name.

Introduction (10 mins): Begin by discussing the importance of names. Explain how names often carry cultural, historical, or personal significance. Share the meanings behind some names, including yours, and how they can reflect heritage, family traditions, or characteristics.

Presentation preparation (15 mins): Give students time to organise their findings. They can create a short presentation, poster, or written explanation about their name's meaning, origin and any cultural or historical connections they discovered.

Sharing (20 mins): Allow students to present their findings to the class. This can be done in pairs or individually, depending on the class size. Encourage them to share any interesting stories or family anecdotes related to their names.

Discussion (10 mins): Discuss the diversity of names and their meanings. Encourage students to reflect on the significance of their own names and what it means to them personally.

Creative work: Students could create a name collage, incorporating images or symbols that represent the meaning or significance of their names. This can be a visual representation of what their names mean to them.

CONCLUSION

In order to keep moving forward, we must learn from the past. History teaches us many lessons, some of which should not be repeated.

In this chapter we looked at different forms of discrimination, ways in which we might discriminate in the classroom, the importance of names and their meanings and the importance of learning lessons from history so that we don't repeat our mistakes.

We have specifically looked at name-based prejudice and discrimination. In order to combat this, it's critical to increase awareness, promote inclusivity and stress the value of respecting people with different names and histories. Important approaches in reducing this kind of prejudice include rules that oppose name-based discrimination, fostering school cultures that promote diversity and having candid conversations about bias and prejudice. It is important to acknowledge and value the cultural significance and distinctiveness of names in order to promote an inclusive and respectful atmosphere in which everyone feels that they belong, regardless of a person's name's origins or associations.

FURTHER READING AND RESOURCES

Your Name is a Song, by Jamilah Thompkins-Bigelow, illustrated by Luisa Uribe

I Am Not a Label: 34 Disabled Artists, Thinkers, Athletes and Activists from Past and Present by Cerrie Burnell, illustrated by Lauren Mark Baldo

Cushing, I. (n.d.) How Black children in England's schools are made to feel like the way they speak is wrong. *The Conversation.* Available at: https://theconversation.com/how-black-children-in-englands-schools-are-made-to-feel-like-the-way-they-speak-is-wrong-198830

Dismantling anti-black linguistic racism in English language arts classrooms: Toward an anti-racist black language pedagogy. *Theory into Practice,* 59(1). Available at: www.tandfonline.com/doi/abs/10.1080/00405841.2019.1665415

Severs, G. (2019) 'No promotion of homosexuality': Section 28 and the No Outsiders protests. *History and Policy.* Available at: www.historyandpolicy.org/policy-papers/papers/no-promotion-of-homosexuality-section-28-and-the-no-outsiders-protests

United Nations (UN) (n.d.) Committee on the Elimination of Racial Discrimination, www.ohchr.org/. Available at: www.ohchr.org/en/treaty-bodies/cerd (Accessed: January 2024)

10

CREATING A WHOLE-SCHOOL CULTURE

KEY CONCEPTS

The key concepts covered in this chapter are:

- what we mean by global citizenship;
- planning for allyship in action;
- how to demonstrate allyship in global citizenship.

INTRODUCTION

The aim of this chapter is to show you how to turn the concept of allyship into a practical part of your school life, reflecting the rich diversity of your school communities. We will share the journey your whole school community will need to embark on together to create a culture of allyship through the concept of global citizenship.

We'll discuss the important steps you can take to ensure that this is not performative, but instead truly embedded within your school culture.

As discussed in the introduction, the approach taken in this book is to embrace all of the diverse cultures and perspectives that are part of our world. I have found that the best way to do this is through the concept of global citizenship. To me, being an active global citizen is about staying open to new ideas and different perspectives and taking actions, big or small, to make the world fairer and more inclusive. This journey lasts a lifetime, and we keep getting better at it as we go, always adapting and growing.

In Chapter 1, we started by talking about how to look after our local community green spaces. If we can teach children how to care for our local neighbourhood, it is easier to teach them the importance of caring for our whole planet.

WHAT IS GLOBAL CITIZENSHIP?

Global citizenship teaches us that we are all part of interconnected communities, no matter where we come from. Becoming a global citizen is like a journey that never ends. It means we keep learning about the world and how we fit into it. We understand that everyone on Earth is connected, and we have a role to play in making the world better.

It is a concept that dates back to a shared desire to avert conflict. It was believed that the more we understood one another, the more likely it was that we could maintain peace, advancement and prosperity. Science has recently made our shared humanity more apparent, bringing us closer together than ever thanks to developments like DNA ancestry testing. DNA ancestry testing is becoming increasingly popular as it not only reveals your genetic heritage, but it also helps an individual to discover their roots and connect with their cultural history. This knowledge fosters a sense of belonging to different cultures and communities, ultimately promoting inclusivity and respect for global diversity.

REFLECTION

Recently I was contacted by one of my foster sisters. Her birth parents are of Caribbean descent. Although she maintains a relationship with her birth mother, she never knew her birth father. She contacted me to say that she had traced back her ancestry, through a DNA test, to Ghana in West Africa, where my family originate from and where my birth parents still live. She told me that she was planning a trip to Ghana. What a lovely surprise it was therefore, to receive an unexpected video call from my mum and dad from their front room in Ghana, with my foster sister sitting there. It made me quite emotional to think that we had been brought up together as foster siblings not knowing that our connection ran deeper than that – we had a shared ancestry.

This understanding of our shared genetic interconnection highlights the fundamental unity of humanity. It encourages us to recognise that we are all part of a broader global family, transcending birth families, local, national and cultural boundaries, and can contribute to a more interconnected and empathetic world.

In a recent interview in *The Voice* newspaper (Mahon, 2022), the founder of UK Black History Month, Akyabba Addai-Sebo, talked about his sense of national pride in its most simplistic form. Addai-Sebo said:

> I am an African who happened to be born in Ghana. I could have been born in the Caribbean. I could have been born in Haiti. I could have been born in Mexico. But I'm an African first. I know who I am as an African. The greatest of all teaching is that man must know thyself, know who you are.

The statement made by Addai-Sebo emphasises a key component of global citizenship. Beyond mentioning the particular nation in which he was born, he underlines his core identity as an African. This idea, which emphasises that people should first acknowledge their shared humanity, regardless of where they were born, reflects a broader concept of global citizenship. Addai-Sebo is a living example of the notion that recognising oneself as a member of a global community is an important feature of global citizenship. It encourages the idea that one's sense of belonging and responsibility to the larger world should not be constrained by our cultural and national identity. In essence, it supports the notion that people who acknowledge their interconnectedness with all of humanity are global citizens, cultivating empathy, inclusivity and a dedication to tackling global concerns.

WHY IS THIS IMPORTANT?

Global citizens are formed, not born. Children gradually come to recognise their common humanity through education from their primary caregivers and other teachers, which helps them to develop a global perspective.

It is imperative to stress the importance of creating a nurturing school culture which is a safe space for every individual within our school community. When people feel safe and encouraged to have open conversations, it is easier to develop as global citizens. This shows the importance of ensuring we build a community that every member feels they belong to.

April Rinne of the *World Economic Forum* describes global citizenship as 'the shared human experience':

> Global citizenship is about the shared human experience. It acknowledges and celebrates that, wherever we come from and wherever we live, we are here together. Our well-being and success are ultimately interdependent. We have more to learn from one another than to fear about our future.
>
> Global citizenship is also about shared values and shared responsibility. [Global citizens] champion fundamental human rights above any national law or identity, and social contracts that preserve elements of equality among all people.
>
> Diversity, interdependence, empathy and perspective are essential values of global citizenship. Global citizens harness these values and are uniquely positioned to contribute in multiple contexts – locally, nationally and internationally – without harming one community to benefit another.
>
> (Rinne, 2017)

ALLYSHIP ACTION PLAN FOR GLOBAL CITIZEN EDUCATION

Using an action plan can help you embed the concepts outlined in this book into a shared understanding across your school. This action plan is designed to prepare children and young people to become informed and engaged global citizens. Like many similar action plans, it consists of two key stages: *preparation* and *development*.

Overall, this action plan aims to equip schools with the knowledge, attitudes and skills necessary to impart in our children so that they become allies in the global effort to combat discrimination, bias and prejudice, and to foster a more inclusive and equitable society.

In the *preparation stage*, teachers are encouraged to raise their awareness by learning about stereotyping, bias and discrimination. They are also urged to engage with people or groups they are not familiar with, fostering empathy and understanding. Moreover, educators are prompted to reassess their assumptions, particularly with regard to perceiving the dominant group as the norm, and examine themselves for prejudices and bias.

We also need to focus on rethinking (pedagogy and curriculum) teaching and learning. This includes reviewing our school's policies and practices to be fairer and making sure we don't just avoid discriminating against marginalised groups but are actively anti-discriminatory.

We want our learning materials to be diverse, covering global topics and including role models from different backgrounds.

The *development stage* focuses on creating a whole-school culture that encourages children to challenge stereotypes by asking questions about what professionals look like. This stage also promotes courageous advocacy so that children feel empowered to challenge stereotypes both within the school and in the media.

Identifying as a pro-equality school is crucial in this stage. Schools are encouraged to make their stance against discrimination clear on their websites and in other communication channels. The implementation of equality schemes is suggested as a means to truly embed these values.

Finally, the action plan urges all members of your school community to actively challenge discrimination, avoid bystander behaviour, educate others and speak out against inequality and injustice. The idea is of being a role model and embodying the personal responsibility of every individual being the change they wish to see in the world.

Table 10.1 Action plan

Preparation stage		
Area of action plan	**How will this be demonstrated?**	**How will we know that this is truly embedded?**
Raise awareness		
Learn about stereotyping, bias and discrimination		
Engage with people or groups who are new to you		
Empathise by considering different perspectives		
Reassess assumptions		
Avoid perceiving the dominant group as the norm		
Self-reflect; both seek and respond to feedback to uncover personal biases		
Audit your school perspective and prejudices with involvement from all stakeholders, including children		
Reassess teaching and learning		
Review policies and practices, emphasising prevention and reporting		

(Continued)

Table 10.1 (Continued)

Preparation stage		
Area of action plan	**How will this be demonstrated?**	**How will we know that this is truly embedded?**
Consider the difference between being non-discriminatory and anti-discriminatory		
Ensure diverse resources and incorporate global issues, like fair trade and suffrage, into subjects		
Promote positive role models Highlight role models from diverse backgrounds, encompassing heritage and gender		
Development stage		
Area of action plan	**How will this be demonstrated?**	**How will we know that this is truly embedded?**
Cultivating a whole-school safe-space culture		
Encourage everyone to question stereotypes: what can a police officer, head teacher, doctor, cleaner, or caretaker look like?		
Foster courage in advocating against stereotypes within the school and in media		
Identify as a pro-equality school		
Clearly communicate your school's anti-racist and anti-sexist stance on the website and other platforms		
Implement equality schemes to support this commitment		
Challenge discrimination		
Refuse to be a bystander in daily life. Act not just as an ally but as an upstander		
Educate others and confront inequality and injustice		
Lead by example, serving as a role model for the change you wish to see		

DEVELOPING AN ALLYSHIP IN GLOBAL CITIZENSHIP FRAMEWORK

Within an allyship in global citizenship framework, students develop the awareness and skills needed to be allies to individuals and communities facing various forms of discrimination or disadvantage. They learn to stand up for the rights and wellbeing of others, from all backgrounds, not just our own. In this way, global citizenship education can serve as a foundation for fostering a culture of allyship, where students are better equipped to support and advocate for equity and justice both locally and globally.

A global citizenship framework typically encompasses several key areas, which help guide the development of a more comprehensive understanding. A framework supports you, as a school, to teach children about the interconnectedness of our world and the importance of being active citizens of our world.

Oxfam has developed a global citizenship framework for schools around a variety of topics related to guiding children towards being global citizens, including *Resources for Schools Speak Out* (Oxfam), supporting young people to demonstrate leadership by speaking out about global poverty and other Oxfam campaigns.

Although Oxfam has not produced any educational content around allyship in particular, it does have a resource, *Teaching Controversial Issues: A Guide for Teachers* (2018), which is helpful in teaching critical thinking skills. An important point contained within their guidance is that: 'Almost any topic can become controversial if individuals or groups offer differing explanations for events, what should happen next or how issues should be resolved' (Oxfam 2018, p. 3).

Oxfam's guidance consists of seven key areas. These are:

1. social justice and equity;
2. identity and diversity;
3. globalisation and interdependence;
4. sustainable development;
5. peace and conflict;
6. human rights;
7. power and governance.

It sets out to teach us the following skills:

- critical and creative thinking;
- empathy;
- self-awareness and reflection;
- communication;

- cooperation and conflict resolution;
- ability to manage complexity and uncertainty;
- informed and reflective action.

At the same time, it aims to teach us values and attitudes around:

- sense of identity and self-esteem;
- commitment to social justice and equity;
- respect for people and human rights;
- valuing diversity;
- concern for the environment and commitment to sustainable development;
- commitment to participation and inclusion;
- belief that people can bring about change.

As a framework it is a good example and is designed to make these 'big ideas' around global citizenship as easy as possible to convert into classroom practice. 'You do not need to be an expert on every global issue to educate your students in global citizenship. Much more important is an ongoing willingness to grapple with what … "big ideas" mean in your classroom practice' (Oxfam, 2015, p. 6).

TEN AREAS TO DEMONSTRATE ALLYSHIP IN GLOBAL CITIZENSHIP

In Table 10.2 we have expanded these seven areas into ten areas to implicitly demonstrate allyship in global citizenship. For each area, it is important to think about the critical thinking skills and empathy development necessary to foster a more inclusive and equitable learning environment.

Table 10.2 Framework for allyship in global citizenship

ALLYSHIP IN GLOBAL CITIZENSHIP		
1. *Cultural awareness and understanding: emphasises valuing diverse cultures*	**Critical thinking skills**	**Empathy development**
This dimension focuses on recognising and appreciating diverse cultures, traditions and worldviews. It encourages respect for different ways of life and the value of cultural diversity	Analyse cultural practices and beliefs critically, considering their historical and social contexts	Seeking to understand the perspectives and experiences of others
2. *Social justice and equity: advocates for fairness and human rights globally*	**Critical thinking skills**	**Empathy development**
Social justice is a core component of allyship in global citizenship. It emphasises the importance of addressing inequalities and advocating for human rights and fairness on a global scale	Evaluate social inequalities, their causes and potential solutions	Empathise with marginalised and disadvantaged groups, recognising their struggles and advocating for their rights
3. *Environmental sustainability: commits to a sustainable world*	**Critical thinking skills**	**Empathy development**
Allyship in global citizenship includes a commitment to environmental responsibility and sustainability. It encourages individuals to consider their impact on the planet and work towards a more sustainable world	Assess the environmental impact of personal and societal actions, seeking sustainable alternatives	Develop a deep connection with nature and empathise with the impact of environmental degradation on future generations
4. *Global interconnectedness: shows how global issues affect everyone*	**Critical thinking skills**	**Empathy development**
Understanding the interconnected nature of our world is vital. This dimension emphasises how global issues, such as climate change or pandemics, affect us all and the importance of international cooperation	Analyse the complex web of global issues, identifying root causes and interdependencies	Cultivate empathy for people around the world affected by global challenges, acknowledging shared responsibilities
5. *Active participation: involves advocacy and civic engagement*	**Critical thinking skills**	**Empathy development**
Allyship in global citizenship is not just about awareness but also about taking active roles in addressing global challenges. This area involves advocacy, volunteering and civic engagement on global issues	Assess the most effective ways to engage in advocacy and civic action	Empathise with those affected by global issues, motivating active involvement in creating positive change

(Continued)

Table 10.2 (Continued)

ALLYSHIP IN GLOBAL CITIZENSHIP		
6. *Critical thinking and problem-solving: encourages problem-solving*	**Critical thinking skills**	**Empathy development**
It encourages individuals to think critically about global problems and develop the skills to find solutions and make informed decisions	Develop problem-solving skills by critically analysing global challenges and proposing innovative solutions	Consider the human impact of problems and prioritise solutions that benefit society as a whole
7. *Intercultural communication: collaborating with diverse backgrounds*	**Critical thinking skills**	**Empathy development**
Effective allyship in global citizenship involves the ability to communicate and collaborate with people from diverse backgrounds, promoting understanding and cooperation	Analyse cross-cultural communication challenges and find strategies to foster effective communication	Deepen cultural understanding, actively listening to others' perspectives and experiences
8. *Ethical responsibility: guided by strong ethics*	**Critical thinking skills**	**Empathy development**
Global citizens often adopt a strong ethical stance, which guides their actions and decisions, ensuring that they contribute to the greater good	Reflect on personal ethics and how they align with global values and responsibilities	Empathise with those facing ethical dilemmas and make ethical decisions that prioritise the greater good
9. *Human rights and human dignity: upholds global human rights*	**Critical thinking skills**	**Empathy development**
This dimension centres on the importance of upholding and advocating for human rights and human dignity on a global scale	Analyse human rights violations and their impact on individuals and societies	Develop a strong empathy for those whose rights are violated and work to advocate for their rights
10. *Peace and conflict resolution: promotes peace and resolution*	**Critical thinking skills**	**Empathy development**
Allyship in global citizenship also includes a commitment to peace and the ability to engage in peaceful conflict resolution	Analyse the root causes of conflicts and develop conflict resolution strategies	Cultivate empathy for those involved in conflicts, seeking peaceful solutions that consider all parties' needs

This framework can be embedded in your wider school curriculum through:

- *integration into core subject areas* through curriculum mapping. At which key points do global citizenship concepts naturally align with your current curriculum content?
- *a cross-disciplinary approach* across the curriculum. Create specific learning outcomes and objectives for global citizenship education across the curriculum;
- *assessment* that explicitly evaluates critical thinking and empathy skills while aligning with the learning objectives and outcomes for global citizenship education;
- *assembly focus points*. Using the framework to incorporate a global citizenship focus into school assemblies through theme-based assemblies, guest speakers and presentations, student-led assemblies, interactive discussions, global awareness challenges and community engagement.

Taking this approach equips students with critical thinking skills and the ability to collaborate with others, preparing them for real-world challenges and contributing to global citizenship. By emphasising allyship, schools nurture compassionate citizens of the future who are committed to social justice and equity, making a lifelong impact on both the school community and the broader world. A whole-school framework ensures that your students are constantly exposed to real-life examples. This is a more effective method than one-off input.

CONCLUSION

Chapter 10 of our journey towards true allyship emphasises the significance of creating a whole-school culture. It sets the stage for turning the concept of allyship into a practical part of daily school life, reflecting the rich diversity present within school communities.

This chapter also emphasises the importance of fostering a whole-school culture that embeds allyship within global citizenship education, preparing students to be active global citizens who understand and respect different cultures and viewpoints, ultimately making the world more inclusive and equitable. It underlines that allyship within global citizenship is an ongoing journey, encouraging individuals to stay open to new ideas, different perspectives and taking actions, big or small, to promote fairness and inclusivity.

We also discussed the idea of recognising one's shared humanity beyond cultural and national identities, emphasising that understanding our interconnectedness is a key feature of global citizenship. It encourages readers to embrace their responsibility towards the larger world, supporting inclusivity and addressing global challenges.

Creating a whole-school culture that truly embeds allyship within the school environment is vital. It's about building a safe and inclusive space where every individual within the school community feels encouraged to have open conversations and feels they belong.

The self-reflection questions underline the importance of open-mindedness, adaptability and a willingness to change one's perspective when new information is learnt.

FURTHER READING AND RESOURCES

FOR ADULTS

Global Citizenship: Engage in the Politics of a Changing World (Inquire and Investigate) (2020) by Julie Knutson, illustrated by Traci Van Wagoner

You Are A Global Citizen: A Guided Journal for the Culturally Curious (2023) by Damon Dominique

How to Raise a Global Citizen: For the Parents of the Children Who Will Save the World (2021) by Anna Davidson, contributions by Marvyn Harrison

Empowering Global Citizens: A World Course (2016) by F.M. Reimers, V. Chopra, C.K. Chung, J. Higdon and E.B. O'Donnell

FOR CHILDREN

We're All Equal (I'm a Global Citizen) (2020) by Georgia Amson-Bradshaw, illustrated by David Broadbent

IDEAS for global citizenship (n.d.) *The Network for Championing Global Citizenship Education in Scotland.* Available at: www.ideas-forum.org.uk/ (Accessed: December 2023)

11

EVERYBODY HAS A ROLE TO PLAY: LIFELONG LEARNING

KEY CONCEPTS

The key concepts covered in this chapter are:

- modelling allyship;
- teaching allyship;
- secret strengths;
- handling difficult conversations.

INTRODUCTION

First of all, let's just say it: allyship is hard!

It undeniably presents challenges and sometimes you might think that you're standing up alone. Being brave necessitates that we actively confront biases and privileges, which can be uncomfortable. Additionally, maintaining allyship demands consistent effort, patience and constant re-education. It's essential to persevere because allyship fosters inclusivity, equality and a more just society. Not being an ally or realising that you have been a victim of performative allyship hurts. Performative allyship carries consequences. It can undermine trust, reinforce harmful stereotypes and impede genuine progress. It massively hinders meaningful change.

I may not be the world's leading authority on allyship, but what I do have is a wealth of painful life experiences that taught me the importance of allyship and how much it meant to me to have someone who stood up for me in that moment that I needed them. These moments underscored the significance of allyship and how a supportive presence made a profound impact when I needed it most. Therefore, I know that, despite its difficulty, persisting as allies is crucial in the fight against injustice and discrimination.

Unfortunately, not everyone shares our belief in the significance of allyship. Differing perspectives exist on this matter, and some may not recognise its importance in fostering inclusivity and social progress. The reasons for scepticism towards allyship can vary. Some individuals might not fully grasp the concept or its potential impact. Others may feel uncomfortable confronting their own biases or may be unaware of systemic injustices. Engaging in open discussions and providing education can help address these concerns and promote a more inclusive perspective. It's important to engage in constructive dialogue and education to encourage a broader understanding of allyship's value.

REFLECTION

In our increasingly interconnected world, modern technology has revolutionised how we communicate, allowing us to engage with a wider range of people and perspectives than ever before. This expansion of communication channels, such as social media, has had a profound impact on my own allyship journey.

As an example, I will share my own learning around a global issue I initially knew very little about, the conflict in Palestine. This is a complex and deeply entrenched issue. I have Muslim and Jewish friends so I wanted to educate myself around this issue so that I could be a better friend and ally to them. I took several steps to learn more about this.

1. *Research*: I began by researching into both the history and current status of the Palestine–Israel conflict. This involved reading articles, following news reports and listening to talk show/podcast discussions to understand the various perspectives and historical background. I am conscious of bias in the media, so I was intentional around widening my news sources. I also used social media to follow people who report directly from the area. However, at the same time, I do not prescribe to hate, therefore I had to ensure that my research aligned with my values.

2. *Engagement*: I joined online forums, discussion groups and attended webinars that featured speakers with diverse viewpoints on the conflict. Engaging with individuals who had first-hand experience and insights helped me appreciate the nuances of the situation.
3. *Advocacy*: To become a more active global citizen, I started advocating for peaceful solutions and humanitarian efforts in the region. I donated to organisations working to provide aid and promote dialogue.
4. *Education*: I furthered my learning through educational resources like documentaries, academic lectures and interviews with experts in the field. This deepened my understanding and allowed me to challenge misconceptions.
5. *Awareness*: I initiated conversations with friends and colleagues about the conflict, sharing information and fostering understanding. However, it was important to me that I asked them how they were feeling about the conflict without being insensitive to their own pain. Asking them directly to educate me about this would have been insensitive.

My journey to understand the Palestine–Israel conflict not only broadened my knowledge but also helped me on my journey to become a more active ally and global citizen. It reinforced to me the interconnectedness of our world and the shared responsibility in addressing global challenges. This is an issue that transcends national borders, as people of Jewish and Muslim faith live across the globe. This experience exemplified the pivotal role that modern technology, including social media, plays in our global citizenship journey, facilitating learning, networking and action on a global scale.

PAUSE FOR SELF-REFLECTION

Think about a world issue that you initially did not know much about.

- How did you educate or re-educate yourself around this issue?
- How did your learning help you to become a more active global citizen?
- What did you learn about yourself and your feelings towards this particular issue?
- Did your opinion change? Why and how?
- How can we prepare our children for the future?

As we've outlined in this book, allyship equips students to handle conflicts peacefully and stand up for fairness and human rights. Coupled with global citizenship, our students learn to understand and respect different cultures and viewpoints, making our society more inclusive. Global citizenship teaches critical thinking about wider global problems, encouraging responsible actions as a response.

HOW DO WE MODEL THIS?

It's important to explain to our children that it's okay to change your mind based on new information. In the previous example of how I educated myself about a global issue, being open to changing our minds is really important. It means that as we discover more about complex global issues, we should be ready to adjust our opinions. By showing this flexibility, we teach our children that it's okay to listen to others and rethink our views. This connects with being open-minded, adaptable and understanding of different perspectives, which are all vital when we deal with global challenges and try to find peaceful solutions. So, changing our minds when we learn new things is an important part of being a good global citizen and, when we show this to our children, we're helping them develop these important qualities too.

HOW DO WE TEACH THIS?

SECRET STRENGTHS

Global citizenship is about knowing that what happens in one place can affect people everywhere. It's like being a good neighbour to everyone on Earth. So, in our school, we're learning to be great global citizens, making the world a better place for everyone. Becoming a global citizen is part of a lifelong journey, not a destination.

Some extraordinary people have made a big difference to our understanding of global citizenship.

- Ban Ki-moon, who used to lead the UN, taught us how important it is to think globally.
- Malala Yousafzai, the young advocate for education, showed us that learning is a key to becoming a global citizen.

- Kofi Annan, a diplomat who also led the UN, talked a lot about global citizenship too.
- Greta Thunberg, a young activist, made everyone aware of how we need to protect the planet and be global citizens to do that.
- Nelson Mandela stood for fairness and justice all around the world.
- Amartya Sen, an economist and thinker, taught us about how development and human rights are part of global citizenship.

These people have shown us how global citizenship is crucial in facing global issues and understanding our shared responsibility. We could refer to them as *thought leaders*, who use thinking as their super-strength. They think deeply about certain important things, and they share those thoughts with the world to help make it a better place. As part of their journey, they would have lots of thinking to do. That doesn't mean they didn't make mistakes along the way. Lots of deep thought would have meant that they changed their mind about certain issues that were important to them, especially when they found out new things, and sometimes changed their minds about what they thought before.

Let's look at a few of the examples of this in more detail.

1. Nelson Mandela was a leader from South Africa who changed his mind about fighting with anger and decided to use peace and understanding to make his country better. He learnt that working together and forgiving each other is very important.
2. Malala Yousafzai is a young hero from Pakistan who changed her mind about staying quiet. At first, she was afraid to speak up about girls' education, but then she realised how important it was. So, she became a brave advocate for girls' rights and education.
3. Greta Thunberg is an ally to the environment. She changed her mind about staying quiet about climate change. She learnt about the environment and decided to talk loudly about it, even if some people didn't like it. Now, she inspires children and adults all over the world to take care of our Earth.
4. Martin Luther King Jr was a hero from the United States who changed his mind about how to fight for fairness. He learnt that peaceful protests and sharing dreams of equality are very strong ways to make the world better.

All these thought leaders teach us that it's okay to change our minds when we learn new things. They show us how important it is to be open to different ideas and work together for a kinder and fairer world. Just like them, we can be global citizens who always want to learn and do better.

It's okay to change your mind in everyday situations too, as long as you have a strong reason to do so and can explain why it is for good. That's our secret strength.

LESSON OR CLASSROOM ACTIVITY

The following activity supports children to understand the idea of changing one's mind, and how it can be a positive thing.

ACTIVITY

CHANGING MINDS FOR A BETTER WORLD

OBJECTIVE

To help children understand the concept of changing one's mind, its importance in global citizenship and its role in making the world a better place.

This activity not only helps children understand the concept of changing one's mind but also reinforces the idea that it's okay and even powerful to do so when new knowledge or understanding comes their way. It instils the values of open-mindedness and adaptability, which are essential for allyship.

MATERIALS NEEDED

- Paper
- Thought cloud outlines

Figure 11.1 Thought cloud outlines

- Coloured pencils or markers

INSTRUCTIONS

1. *Introduction* (10 minutes):

Begin by discussing the idea of changing one's mind and how it can lead to positive changes in the world. Use the examples of the thought leaders given or choose others that reflect current discussions within the class which also illustrate the power of changing one's perspective for the better.

2. *Storytelling* (10 minutes):

Choose one of the thought leaders and tell a short, age-appropriate story about a time they changed their mind and how it made a positive impact. You can use storytelling props or visual aids to make the story engaging. Add an example of when you, as an adult, changed your mind about an important issue.

3. *Group discussion* (10 minutes):

- Engage the children in a discussion about times when they have changed their minds. Ask questions like: can you think of a time when you used to believe something, but then you learnt something new that made you change your mind?
- How did changing your mind affect your actions or the way you interacted with others?
- Can you share a positive experience where changing your mind led to a better outcome?

Note: Please be sensitive to maturity levels and stories such as the tooth fairy, Father Christmas etc. and recognise that some children may be sensitive to this. Also ensure that you are respectful to religious beliefs.

4. *Art activity* (20 minutes):

Provide each child with paper and coloured pencils or markers. Ask them to draw two large thought clouds on opposite sides of a piece of paper. In the thought clouds ask them to write about a time when they changed their mind and how it made a difference. Encourage them to be creative and use their imagination, using pictures and key words if they prefer.

They could also draw a picture of themselves, an open mind or a brain between the thought clouds.

5. *Sharing* (10 minutes):

Invite all children to share their drawings or stories with the group. This is an opportunity for them to express themselves and learn from each other's experiences.

6. *Reflection* (5 minutes):

- Conclude the activity with a brief reflection. Ask the children: how did it feel to share your experience of changing your mind?
- Why is it important to be open to new ideas and willing to change our minds?
- How can changing our minds help us become better global citizens?

7. *Secret strengths* (5 minutes):

Remind the children that changing their minds when they learn new things is one of their secret strengths. Encourage them to continue being open to different ideas and working together for a kinder and fairer world.

HANDLING DIFFICULT CONVERSATIONS ABOUT ALLYSHIP AND THE BYSTANDER EFFECT

Throughout this book we have discussed how we can create an atmosphere in our classrooms and our homes that allows for open discussion and challenge so that children can learn and re-learn how to be effective allies. We have explored concepts of allyship and bystander awareness through the use of sensitive and empathetic strategies.

We have discussed the importance of:

- *creating a safe environment* so that we can promote respect and active listening;
- *discussing* the why so that we are able to explore abstract concepts;
- *encouraging self-reflection* so that we use our feelings around our own personal experiences to create connections;
- *addressing feelings of discomfort* and acknowledging that we may feel uncomfortable, but we need to sit with this in order to confront prejudice;
- *giving space* for children to express their opinions and answering their questions with empathy;
- *fostering critical thinking* through scenarios and stories around allyship and the bystander effect;
- *emphasising kindness* so that we all begin to understand the importance of empathy and considering the feelings and needs of others;
- *exploring strategies* and providing resources of tried and tested methods while also allowing children to share their own ideas;
- *emphasising* that we are all *lifelong learners*, and we don't all get it right – but we learn and use our mistakes for opportunities to do better. Growth takes time.

These conversations are ongoing and will require further discussions. It is a good idea to dip in and out of this book when needed, especially if incidents of bullying, discrimination or harassment occur again.

It is important to remember that conversations need to be ongoing. It is also vitally important to maintain an open dialogue where children and young people feel able to ask questions, feed back on what they have been taught and change their minds about their initial thinking. As educators it is our job to give our children and young people ongoing support as they navigate their journey to allyship. This is not a one-off conversation – it can't be, that doesn't work. What works is a commitment to revisiting this topic over and over again as part of a lifelong journey.

COMMON QUESTIONS AND SUGGESTED ANSWERS

Below are common questions with suggested answers – the former to help children check their understanding and the latter to help you, as educators and parents/carers, to reinforce change. These questions offer an opportunity to engage in meaningful conversations, so it is important not to shut children down when they ask them. Being a child is about being curious, so encourage and guide children to explore answers for themselves. The suggested answers here are to help parents/carers and educators reinforce the importance of being an ally and fostering empathy.

1. *What does it mean to be an ally?*

   Answer: Being an ally means that you support and stand up for someone who is facing challenges, discrimination, or bullying. It means being a friend who helps and cares for others, especially when they need it most.

2. *Why is it important to help others if they're in trouble?*

   Answer: It's important to help others in trouble because it shows kindness and compassion. When we help, we make the world a better place, and we become part of a community where people look out for one another.

3. *What stops people from helping someone in need?*

   Answer: Sometimes, people might be afraid of getting involved or worried about what others will think. It's important to remember that helping others is a courageous and kind act.

4. *How can you be a good friend and help others when they're bullied or sad?*

   Answer: To be a good friend, you can lend a listening ear, offer comfort and stand up against bullying. Sometimes, just being there for someone and letting them know you care can make a big difference.

5. *Can I be an ally even if I'm shy or quiet?*

   Answer: Yes, absolutely! Being an ally doesn't always mean being loud or outspoken. You can be a quiet but strong support for your friends by being there when they need you and showing kindness.

6. *What should I do if I see someone being treated unfairly?*

   Answer: If you witness someone being treated unfairly, you can step in and stand up for them. Let them know you're there to support them and report the unfair treatment to a trusted adult.

7. *How do I know when to step in and help and when to stay out of it?*

   Answer: Trust your instincts. If you see someone being hurt, bullied, or treated unfairly, it's generally a good idea to step in and help. If it's not safe to intervene directly, seek help from a trusted adult.

8. *What if I want to help, but I'm scared of getting in trouble too?*

   Answer: It's natural to feel scared, but remember that seeking help from adults or teachers is an important way to address a situation without getting into trouble. Safety should always come first.

9. *Can I be an ally for someone who is different from me?*

   Answer: Yes, you can be an ally for anyone, regardless of the differences. Being an ally means showing kindness and support to all people, no matter their background or identity.

10. *What if someone tells me to mind my own business? Should I still help?*

    Answer: It's essential to consider the situation. If someone is in danger or being hurt, it's better to seek help from an adult. However, in less severe cases, respecting their request and notifying an adult can be a good approach.

11. *How can I encourage my friends to be better allies too?*

    Answer: You can lead by example and show your friends how to be good allies. Talk to them about kindness, respect and standing up for what's right.

12. *What's the difference between being an ally and just being nosy?*

    Answer: Being an ally means helping when someone needs it, while being nosy is about being overly curious about someone's personal business without their permission. Being respectful and helping is different from invading someone's privacy.

13. *Have there been times in history when people didn't help others and it caused problems?*

    Answer: Yes, history has shown instances where people didn't help, leading to serious problems. Learning from these historical events reminds us of the importance of being allies and standing up for what's right.

14. *What can I say if someone is being mean to my friend because of their race or background?*

    Answer: You can say something like, 'That's not fair, and it's not kind to judge someone based on their race or background.' You can also let them know that you're there to support your friend.

15. *I'm only a child; can I really make a difference in stopping bullying or helping others?*

    Answer: Yes, even as a child, you can make a big difference. Your kindness, support and actions can inspire others to do the same. Remember, positive change often starts with small acts of kindness.

CONCLUSION

Fostering allyship involves feeling comfortable with open discussions and challenging conversations. To get to this point, it's essential to create a safe environment for respectful and empathetic discussions. Encouraging self-reflection and addressing discomfort in these conversations are vital steps in raising thoughtful and compassionate individuals.

Changing one's mind and being open to new information is a significant aspect of allyship and the bystander effect. It's essential to encourage children to explore answers and adapt their perspectives as they learn and grow. Our children are all leaders of tomorrow.

Lifelong learning is a continuous process, that's why it's called *lifelong*. Therefore, children should feel free to ask questions and adjust their views as they learn and reflect.

Common questions children may have about allyship are opportunities for meaningful discussions. These discussions will be ongoing, not only as our children learn, but as we do too.

KEY TAKE AWAYS

I wrote this book after a painful experience of discrimination, therefore doing so has been a therapeutic outlet for me. It's a shame that experiencing discrimination first hand was the push I needed to take more affirmative action to ensure change. The most important lesson I have learnt while writing this book, is that we all have the power to make a difference and as educators we make a difference every single day to every single student we teach. We inspire change through our daily interactions. That's a lot of responsibility and, more often than not, that means stepping out of our comfort zone and being a little braver – but if we don't, nothing changes. We are role models to our students and our peers. I think about all the people that have come before me and all the people committing to continuing to do the work now. This often involves navigating hostile environments, but they persevere, we persevere because our children deserve better, we deserve better. We deserve to live a life where we are able to fulfil our individual potential. We may need some help to achieve this, but that's what allyship is about.

Thank you for reading this book, for being a true ally and not a bystander, and for your ongoing commitment to nurturing the next generation, all of our children, to be global citizens.

Now it's over to you to carry on the work.

Take some time to:

- sum up the key takeaways from this book;
- reflect on what you've learnt and how you plan to apply it in your own life.

Feel free to contact me at www.inclusionht.com

REFERENCES

Abbas, R. (2023) Why your business isn't a 'family'. *Recruiting Resources: How to Recruit and Hire Better*. Available at: https://resources.workable.com/stories-and-insights/business-isnt-family (Accessed: December 2023)

Akinde, F. (2023) My brand identity AKINDAT. Available at: https://inclusionht.wordpress.com/2023/01/17/my-brand-identity-akindat/ (Accessed: December 2023)

Angelo, M. (2014) 16 Unforgettable things Maya Angelou wrote and said. *Glamour*. Available at: www.glamour.com/story/maya-angelou-quotes (Accessed: March 2024)

Anti-Bullying Alliance (n.d.) False friendships. Available at: https://anti-bullyingalliance.org.uk/tools-information/all-about-bullying/what-bullying/false-friendships (Accessed: December 2023)

ASCL (2020) Public Sector Equality Duty (PSED) Guidance Paper. Available at: www.ascl.org.uk/ASCL/media/ASCL/Help%20and%20advice/Leadership%20and%20governance/Guidance-paper-Public-Sector-Equality-Duty.pdf (Accessed: December 2023)

Baldwin, J. (2017) Culture, prejudice, racism, and discrimination. *Oxford Research Encyclopedia of Communication*. Available at: https://oxfordre.com/communication/display/10.1093/acrefore/9780190228613.001.0001/acrefore-9780190228613-e-164 (Accessed: December 2023)

BBC News (2022) Child Q: Strip-search Met police officers facing gross misconduct case. Available at: www.bbc.co.uk/news/uk-england-london-61796798 (Accessed: December 2023)

Bryan, J.H. and Test, M.A. (1967) Models and helping: Naturalistic studies in aiding behavior. *Journal of Personality and Social Psychology*, 6(4, Pt1), 400–7. Available at: https://doi.org/10.1037/h0024826

Crenshaw, K. (1991) Mapping the margins: Intersectionality, identity politics, and violence against women of color. *Stanford Law Review*, 43(6), 1241–1299. https://doi.org/10.2307/1229039

DeCuir-Gunby, J.T. and Bindra, V.G. (2022) How does teacher bias influence students? An introduction to the special issue on teachers' implicit attitudes, instructional practices, and student outcomes, *Learning and Instruction*, 78, 101523, ISSN 0959-4752

Department for Education (DfE) (2018) *Equality Act 2010: Advice for Schools*. Available at: www.gov.uk/government/publications/equality-act-2010-advice-for-schools (Accessed: December 2023)

DfE (2019) *Education (Independent School Standards) Regulations 2014*. Available at: https://assets.publishing.service.gov.uk/media/5cd3fc2fe5274a3fd6ee74b0/Independent_School_Standards-_Guidance_070519.pdf (Accessed: February 2024)

DfE (2020) *Teaching about Mental Wellbeing*. Available at: www.gov.uk/guidance/teaching-about-mental-wellbeing (Accessed: December 2023)

DfE (2021a) *Relationships and Sex Education (RSE) and Health Education*. Available at: www.gov.uk/government/publications/relationships-education-relationships-and-sex-education-rse-and-health-education (Accessed: December 2023)

DfE (2021b) *Promoting and Supporting Mental Health and Wellbeing in Schools and Colleges*. Available at: www.gov.uk/guidance/mental-health-and-wellbeing-support-in-schools-and-colleges (Accessed: December 2023)

DfE (2023a) *Permanent Exclusions*. Available at: www.ethnicity-facts-figures.service.gov.uk/education-skills-and-training/absence-and-exclusions/permanent-exclusions/latest/ (Accessed: January 2023)

DfE (2023b) *Suspension and Permanent Exclusion Guidance*. Available at: https://assets.publishing.service.gov.uk/media/64ef773513ae1500116e30db/Suspension_and_permanent_exclusion_guidance_september_23.pdf (Accessed: January 2024)

DfE (2023c) *Keeping Children Safe in Education*. Available at: www.gov.uk/government/publications/keeping-children-safe-in-education–2 (Accessed: December 2023)

DfE (2023d) *Parent First Approach at the Core of New Guidance on Gender Questioning Children*. Available at: www.gov.uk/government/news/parent-first-approach-at-the-core-of-new-guidance-on-gender-questioning-children (Accessed: December 2023)

Dr Seuss (1954) *Horton Hears a Who!* London: Random House.

Dr Seuss (1971) *The Lorax*. London: Random House.

Equality Act 2010 (2010) Available at: www.legislation.gov.uk/ukpga/2010/15/contents (Accessed: December 2023).

Foreign, Commonwealth and Development Office (FCDO) (2018) *Connecting Classrooms Through Global Learning*. Available at: www.gov.uk/international-development-funding/connecting-classrooms (Accessed: January 2024)

Government Equalities Office (GEO) (2018) *National LGBT Survey: Research Report*. Manchester: GEO. Available at: https://assets.publishing.service.gov.uk/media/5b3b2d1eed915d33e245fbe3/LGBT-survey-research-report.pdf (Accessed: March 2024)

GOV.UK (2015) *Bullying at School*. Available at: www.gov.uk/bullying-at-school (Accessed: December 2023)

Hallahan, G. (2021) The assessment bias trap: What the tags taught us. *Tes Magazine*. Available at: www.tes.com/magazine/news/secondary/assessment-bias-trap-what-tags-taught-us (Accessed: December 2023)

Hubbard, L. (2021) *The Hate Crime Report 2021: Supporting LGBT+ Victims of Hate Crime*. London: Galop. Available at: https://galop.org.uk/wp-content/uploads/2021/06/Galop-Hate-Crime-Report-2021-1.pdf (Accessed: December 2023)

Human Rights Act 1998 (1998) Available at: www.legislation.gov.uk/ukpga/1998/42/contents (Accessed: December 2023)

Just Like Us (2021) *Growing Up LGBT+: The Impact of School, Home and Coronavirus on LGBT+ Young People*. Available at: www.justlikeus.org/wp-content/uploads/2021/11/Just-Like-Us-2021-report-Growing-Up-LGBT.pdf (Accessed: December 2023)

Luthra, R. and Nandi, A. (2022) *Is Hate Crime Rising During the Covid-19 Crisis?* Institute for Social and Economic Research (ISER). Available at:

www.iser.essex.ac.uk/blog/2020/07/29/is-hate-crime-rising-during-the-covid-19-crisis (Accessed: December 2023)

Mahon, L. (2022) The man who started Black History Month. *Voice Online*. Available at: www.voice-online.co.uk/news/history/2022/10/02/the-man-who-started-black-history-month/ (Accessed: December 2023)

Mahon, L. (2023) Just 1 in 10 Black Brits are 'definitely proud to be British'. *Voice Online*. Available at: www.voice-online.co.uk/black-british-voices/2023/09/28/just-1-in-10-black-brits-are-definitely-proud-to-be-british/ (Accessed: December 2023)

McDougall, G. (2021) *The International Convention on the Elimination of All Forms of Racial Discrimination*. United Nations Audiovisual Library of International Law. Available at: https://legal.un.org/avl/pdf/ha/cerd/cerd_e.pdf (Accessed: November 2023)

Ministry of Justice (MOJ) (2012) *Public Sector Equality Duty*. Available at: www.gov.uk/government/publications/public-sector-equality-duty (Accessed: December 2023)

Mulvey, K.L., Gönültaş, S., Goff, E., Irdam, G., Carlson, R., DiStefano, C. and Irvin, M. (2019) School and family factors predicting adolescent cognition regarding bystander intervention in response to bullying and victim retaliation. *Journal of Youth and Adolescence*, 48, 581–596. https://doi.org/10.1007/s10964-018-0941-3

Nagesh, A. (2022) Hate crimes recorded by police up by more than a quarter. *BBC News*. Available at: www.bbc.co.uk/news/uk-63157965 (Accessed: December 2023)

Newton, P. (2021) Bias in teacher assessment results. *The Ofqual Blog*. Available at https://ofqual.blog.gov.uk/2021/05/17/bias-in-teacher-assessment-results/(Accessed: December 2023)

Nielson, L.A. (2018) *Nature's Allies: Eight Conservationists Who Changed Our World*. Washington, DC: Island Press.

Nordell, J. (2022) *The End of Bias: Can We Change Our Minds?* London: Granta.

Ofsted and Spielman, A. (2019) *HMCI Commentary: Managing Behaviour Research*. Available at: www.gov.uk/government/speeches/research-commentary-managing-behaviour (Accessed: December 2023)

Oxfam (2015) *Global Citizenship in the Classroom: A Guide for Teachers.* Available at: https://oxfamilibrary.openrepository.com/bitstream/handle/10546/620105/edu-global-citizenship-teacher-guide-091115-en.pdf (Accessed: December 2023)

Oxfam (2018) *Teaching Controversial Issues: A Guide for Teachers.* Available at: https://oxfamilibrary.openrepository.com/bitstream/handle/10546/620473/gd-teaching-controversial-issues-290418-en.pdf (Accessed: December 2023)

Oxfam (n.d.) *Resources for Schools Speak Out.* Available at: www.oxfam.org.uk/education/get-involved/start-oxfam-school-group/resources-oxfam-school-groups/ (Accessed: December 2023)

Project Implicit (n.d.) *Implicit Association Test (IAT).* Available at: https://implicit.harvard.edu/implicit/takeatest.html (Accessed: December 2023)

PSHE Association (n.d.) *Build Your Programme.* Available at: https://pshe-association.org.uk/guidance/ks1-5/planning/build-your-programme (Accessed: December 2023)

Right To Be (n.d.) *The 5Ds of Bystander Intervention.* Available at: https://righttobe.org/guides/bystander-intervention-training/ (Accessed: December 2023)

Rinne, A. (2017) What is global citizenship? *World Economic Forum.* Available at: www.weforum.org/agenda/2017/11/what-is-global-citizenship/ (Accessed: December 2023)

Roberts, N. and Bolton, P. (2023) *Educational Outcomes of Black Pupils and Students.* House of Commons Library. Available at: https://researchbriefings.files.parliament.uk/documents/CBP-9023/CBP-9023.pdf (Accessed: December 2023)

Robinson, J., Espelage, D. and Rivers, I. (2013) Developmental trends in peer victimization and emotional distress in LGB and heterosexual youth. *Pediatrics,* 131. 10.1542/peds.2012-2595

Sanderson, C.A. (2022) *Why We Act: Turning Bystanders into Moral Rebels.* Cambridge, MA: Belknap.

Stonewall (2017) *School Report 2017.* Available at: www.stonewall.org.uk/resources/school-report-2017 (Accessed: January 2024)

Studte, S., Clement, M., Soliman, M. and Boenigk, S. (2019) Blood donors and their changing engagement in other prosocial behaviors. *Transfusion*, 59(3), 1002–15. doi: 10.1111/trf.15085. Epub 2018 Dec 14. PMID: 30549293. Available at: https://pubmed.ncbi.nlm.nih.gov/30549293/

Suzy Lamplugh Trust (2022) *Anti-harassment Training*. Available at: www.suzylamplugh.org/anti-harassment-training (Accessed: December 2023)

Teachly (n.d.) Available at: https://teachly.me/ (Accessed: December 2023)

Tidman, Z. (2020) Gypsy, traveller and Black Caribbean pupils 'twice as likely to be permanently excluded from school'. *Independent*. Available at: www.independent.co.uk/news/education/education-news/gypsy-roma-traveller-black-carribbean-permanent-exclusions-school-dfe-figure-a9646561.html (Accessed: January 2024)

UN (1965) *International Convention on the Elimination of All Forms of Racial Discrimination*. Availiable at: www.ohchr.org/en/instruments-mechanisms/instruments/international-convention-elimination-all-forms-racial (Accessed: March 2024)

UNESCO and Global Education Monitoring Report Team (2022) #HerEducationOurFuture #BreakTheBias: challenging gender bias and stereotypes in and through education; the latest facts on gender equality in education. UNESCO Digital Library. Available at: https://unesdoc.unesco.org/ark:/48223/pf0000380827 (Accessed: December 2023)

UNICEF (2023) Discussing war and conflict in class. Rights Respecting Schools Award. Available at: www.unicef.org.uk/rights-respecting-schools/resources/teaching-resources/guidance-assemblies-lessons/discussing-war-and-conflict-in-class/ (Accessed: December 2023)

United Nations Convention on the Rights of the Child (UNCRC) (1989) 20 November, 1577 U.N.T.S. 3.

Vassell, N. (2020) 'Like death by a thousand cuts': How microaggressions play a traumatic part in everyday racism. *Independent*. Available at: www.independent.co.uk/life-style/microaggression-meaning-definition-racism-black-lives-matter-george-floyd-a9568506.html (Accessed: December 2023)

Vassell, N. (2023) Shola Mos-Shogbamimu praised for making Dawn Neesom pronounce her name correctly on live TV. *Independent*. Available at: www.independent.co.uk/arts-entertainment/tv/news/shola-mos-shogbamimu-jeremy-vine-dawn-neesom-b2336352.html (Accessed: December 2023).

INDEX